A Tattoo to Die For

(A Monk Johnson Mystery Story)

By

Jim McGarrah

ISBN: 978-93-95131-04-9

First Edition: 2022
Rs. 200/-

Rochak Publishing
HIG 45 Kaushambi Kunj, Kalindipuram
Allahabad - 211011 (U.P.) India
http://www.rochakpublishing.com
Tel: +(91) 9415091004
E-mail: info@rochakpublishing.com

Printed in India at VORE LLP.

Dedicated to my friends who understand

the mystery in being human - Tom Wilhelmus and Ron Mitchell

This is the way the world ends
This is the way the world ends
This is the way the world ends
Not with a bang but a whimper.

—T.S. Eliot

Contents

Headline: You Don't Have to be a Detective to Hate a Detective

Security Guard Monk Johnson was always wary when the phone rang late at night. No one ever called at this hour to say you won the lottery or your grandma got over her heart attack. His first wife rang him up one midnight and told him she wasn't coming home—ever. A 1 AM phone alert roused him from a solid sleep to cover the U.S. embassy in Saigon. Of course, the call came on Tet, 1968. No, he felt very uncomfortable picking up the receiver, but did so reluctantly in fear that it might be a supervisor checking up on him and Frank.

"Backstretch guard shack, Churchill Downs racetrack. Can I help you?"

A voice filtered through static.

"You order a pizza?"

"What?"

"What? A pizza. I got a large pepperoni here, and I ain't sending out my driver unless you ordered it."

For a minute, Monk felt lost.

"Who is this?"

"Domino's. Yes, or no?"

"What's the name on it."

"Frank at the racetrack is all the ticket says."

Okay, so it could have been worse. But Frank better pay for it.

"How much?"

"Five dollars and eighty-six cents with tax."

"Yeah, send it on."

He contacted Frank on the walky-talky and told him to get his butt in gear. Monk would stand a round of drinks, loan someone bus fare, buy an indigent breakfast, but no way was he going to pay for Frank's prodigious snack habits. The man would come to work with a bag full of Moby Dick's batter-fried fish from across the street, order something else for delivery before his first break, and save his lunch pail full of stuff his wife cooked for the wee hours. It was okay to weigh three hundred pounds if you were six foot six inches tall, but Frank was five foot six.

Monk's nightshift partner, Frank Morello, arrived with a waddle as he finished walking the barn area on his rounds. At least, Monk thought of it as a waddle. Frank always seemed to be catching up with his belly before it toppled him to the ground. The belly came first pulling the man's chest and head forward and down. Then, he slid a leg underneath the great gelatinous mass, first one and then another, and moved ahead slowly. You could almost imagine a delicate balance and grace in his movements. A stumbling, bumbling, rumbling ballet of sorts, thought Monk. As Frank pushed the guard shack door open and squeezed through, a dark blue Ford sedan pulled up in front of the gate. Monk side-stepped a wheezing Frank and glided past him onto the pavement in front of the horsemen's backside entrance to the barn area.

"I got this, big boy. You catch your breath before you have a stroke."

"Is it my pizza?" asked Frank.

"Not unless the Louisville PD delivers Domino's."

A zone exists when there is no time, as such. Night has passed and day is floating in a sort of cosmic stasis. People awake to this pre-dawn gray unsure if the world around them is real or a dream, unsure if the images in their minds exist outside of the mind. To escape this limbo and move forward into light, thoughts must be jolted away from themselves and connect with external senses. Some people do it with alarm clocks, others with loud music or cold water on the face.

These ideas occupied Monk's mind during this night shift. Since coming to work as a security guard at the world-famous home of the Kentucky Derby strange and groggy reflections were part of his regular AM routine. He called them random insanities. Monk, not asleep, but in that in-between zone, needed help connecting with wokeness. He got it. A white-haired man in a short-sleeved white shirt and a tie thrust a deeply tanned arm out of the driver's side open window. In his hand he held a gold detective shield. The man spoke gruffly and with the authority of someone whose years on the job demanded respect.

"Do you recognize this man?"

The detective, who had yet to identify himself, stuck a wrinkled Polaroid photo in Monk's face. Instantly, the guard remembered Red Harvey's wedding day and how the groom had grabbed him and pulled him close while Bobby Burchell, a horse trainer, snapped the picture. It was a wedding from the fall race meet the year before and right after he had been hired. Monk winced.

"Who are you?"

"He's a cop, a real one," said Frank, following Monk out of the guard shack.

"That much is obvious. Why don't you go finish the night reports and leave us to my personal business here, whatever it is."

Frank stumbled off. The cop turned the picture over, and Monk saw some chicken scratches on the back that he conjectured to be writing. With his other hand, the officer pointed to the badge now clipped on his belt.

"My name is Detective Joe Phelps."

"Your first name is Detective?"

"Cut the crap and answer my question."

As he squinted under the blanched glow of the street light overhead scratches began to focus and separate into letters. Monk made out the few words—*Me, Monk Johnson, and Billy Chernov, my best man. Churchill Downs, 1972*. In the right corner blow the written caption Monk noticed an insignificant scribble, *Z59324*. The letters and numbers could signify a thousand different thinks or nothing at all. Phelps never mentioned them.

"Yeah, yeah…that's Red Harvey."

"When's the last time you saw him?"

"A couple of days ago. He was coming back to the track after getting drunk somewhere. The bus from Fourth and Market makes a stop by this gate."

"You sure that's the last time you saw him?"

Monk wasn't stupid, although people often treated him that way because he lived by himself, worked a minimum wage job, and drank too much. Not many people understood how a war affected your outlook on the future, made you just want to live day by day and be left alone. Monk Johnson lived exactly the way he wanted to, with very little responsibility and where his two ex-wives couldn't find him. He didn't see himself as a bookish man, but he was an avid reader. He scanned the Courier Journal most mornings and considered the Daily Racing Form the way most Christians thought of the Bible, as a sacred text that guided the faithful successfully through life. When he stumbled on a good paperback, he would sit for hours beneath the bare bulb over his bed at Jody's Sleeping Rooms on 5th Street and read till his eyes watered so much he had to quit. In this way, he felt as if he were keeping something that resembled humanity. He forced himself to be literate. Two books proved to be his all-time favorites, *Catch-22*, which he had read while recuperating from his wounds at Camp Drake Army Hospital in 1968 and the brand new one he had just finished in three days, *The World According to Garp*. He saw a situation coming from the cop that could have been a scene in either one, some crazy, random event completely out of his control and involving Red Harvey. What had Red's glib tongue gotten him into this time?

"Well, I sure as hell don't socialize with him. He's just one of a dozen drunks in the barn area who hotwalks racehorses to earn whiskey money."

"And you haven't seen him since, right?"

"Jesus, I said no once already."

The more the detective pressed the issue, the more Monk saw the waters of an undertow current closing over him. Sucked down by the current, he struggled with the same sensation of helplessness that overwhelmed him when he joined into the army. This was proving itself a good morning to get drunk. The cop extracted another photo from his folder. This one was black and white.

"How about this picture? Recognize this guy?"

Monk sucked in air with a slight, but audible gasp. The cop noticed and smiled. The corpse on the slab appeared to be Red Harvey. Swelling and gashes and skinned areas, as if the body had been dragged over hard ground, made a definite identification difficult. But there was no denying the bald head with a red hair halo. For a moment his stomach rose into his throat as if he had just crested a hill too fast in his truck. Then, he focused on his composure, trying not to give anymore of himself away to the detective who was obviously looking for suspects.

"Might be old Red. What happened?"

"Patrol car found him in an alley around Market Street, not far from Jefferson College, about two in the morning. Looked like he'd been victim of a hit and run or beat to a pulp by something. He had a racetrack ID in his pocket. You here all night?"

"All night. I got witnesses enough for that, and there's my pickup truck over there. It's got plenty of dents and scrapes but none of them made by flesh and bone."

"I figured you to be here all night. I was just checking to make sure you had an alibi. I need to get a positive ID on the body. We couldn't find anything on him to indicate any emergency contact or if he had a next of kin."

"He didn't have any family as far as I know."

"Then I guess it falls to you to make a personal identification." Joe Phelps removed a small notepad from his shirt pocket and wrote a name, Dr. Richard Greathouse. Handing the paper to Monk, he said, "Go by the coroner's office before noon and ask for the doc here. Tell him I sent you. We need official conformation whether or not this is Red Harvey. You got any idea where the coroner's office is?"

"I told you already, I barely knew the guy, and we weren't buddies."

Detective Phelps smirked. Monk had no notion whatsoever where the office was, but there was no way Phelps would get the satisfaction.

"I'm not as stupid as I look."

It was a government office. It stood to reason it would be in with all the other offices downtown on Broadway at the municipal government building. After the police cruiser left the area, the security guard took a moment to consider things. Had Red stumbled into traffic and been struck by a car? That would mean he fell off the dry wagon and gotten plastered again. Nothing unusual there. Were those cuts and bruises the result of a fight with someone Red had pissed off by cheating at cards or by just being his annoying little self? Were the police simply trying to identify another vagrant so they could put a name on their case file and close it out fast? He had learned not to accept too much of anything at face value anymore. What if Red's death might not be as simple as the cops wanted to make. Sure, it would be easy to close the case on a nobody drunk who died wondering around a neighborhood he should've stayed out of, and maybe it was just a rose, like that writer once said. "A rose is a rose is a rose."

But the little hotwalker was a stubborn bastard. Red seemed determined to dry out for good this last time he made the effort. He must have wanted to. If not, why put himself through the agony of the track Chaplin's rehab for Jesus program? Monk forgot to ask if Red could have been drunk and stumbled into traffic, but the cop was long gone. A quick wave of pity flushed over him. Then, he remembered that Red lived longer than a lot of guys he knew in 'Nam and many of them had a lot more to live for. Shit happens. A tumor, a bullet, a car wreck, a heart attack, eventually everyone hits that last immovable wall, and like a bird that flies into a plate glass window, most people never see it coming. Shit happens. Red had stepped in a pile of shit and one of these days, so would he.

Still, a tiny electric current of curiosity shot through his nervous system and raised goose bumps on his bare arms. It wasn't an altogether unpleasant feeling. As a matter of fact, he felt more alive since glancing at the photo than he had for months, maybe years. Only a person completely dead inside wouldn't want answers for how and why this death came about. It was a mystery. Who didn't love a good mystery? Monk wasn't dead inside, just badly damaged. Also, he was hungry. He couldn't face the morgue without his usual breakfast.

Headline: Sometimes a Home Has Bars and Sometimes Bars Are Home

In a world made from shadows and magic there are two types of bars. One type covers windows or forms cages, but the best bars serve whiskey. Whatever type of bar you have in mind it was probably created to hold some men in and protect them from the rest of the world or to protect the rest of the world from them. It depended on the man. Monk Johnson had grown familiar with both types, and the idea of remaining isolated from most of the assholes that populated the world was a strong motivation for either. He found that the bars serving whiskey served him best. They gave him control over his associates and his environment. He chose those habitats populated sparsely and by cynical, innocuous, little people whose expertise consisted of drinking seriously and mostly in silence.

Monk's personal sanctuary happened to be located just off 5th Street about two minutes from the back gate of Churchill Downs racetrack and one minute from his sleeping room. He drove by it one Sunday morning the year before when he first began working for the management at the racetrack as a security guard. Hungover and remorseful for drinking on the job, he left the track in search of a place to atone for his weakness. Monk took the tavern's name to be a prophetic sign, J.C.'s Bar & Grill. Any place with Jesus Christ's initials that houses so many wonderful spirits, must be the right spot for a sinner.

He stood outside the screen door for a couple of minutes smoking a Lucky Strike and watching and listening to the life within. To the best of his knowledge, no other place poured drinks as early as 7 a.m. Beyond that, breakfast was cheap and the coffee good. He recognized the two voices from within. One was the bartender and owner. His name was

Charlie, a chubby man, short and soft with a pockmarked face. His hair, parted in the middle and pasted down both sides of his slightly large head, resembled a dark oil stain that shifted *enmasse* when he spoke. His face always seemed dirty as the result of not shaving for several days at a time. The other man, a racetrack bum who mucked stalls for a few dollars named Victor, looked old, his face worn smooth and thin like a stone in a riverbed that remained unmoved for centuries while life flowed over it. But his appearance may have been more a result of lifestyle rather than age. Monk often felt much older that his years himself. He opened the screen door and followed three flies inside.

Neatly dressed and clean in a white shirt, black trousers, and a red silk tie, Victor nursed a glass of Falls City beer from atop a barstool that seemed to be part of his anatomy. Charlie wiped the countertop with a brown stained bar towel in slow circular motions.

"I ain't seen the place this empty since Dutch gave away free Sicilian pizza at the cafeteria last Christmas," said Monk.

"I say… and it tasted like someone mailed it from Sicily on a slow boat," Victor responded as he lifted his glass to drain it.

"Well, you know Dutch. Tighter than bark on a tree. He don't waste nothing," Charlie added.

"I say… that somabitch was never one to waste money on fresh ingredients, especially if he's giving them away."

"Or, if he's charging an arm and a leg for them either," said Charlie. "Another beer?"

Victor slid his glass toward Charlie. "One more. Then I gotta go."

"What about you Monk, the usual?"

Charlie picked the glass up and tossed it into the suds filled sink. Taking a semi-clean one from the shelf, he shoved it under the tap and drew another beer.

"Yeah, only put a shot of Jim Beam in the coffee today and tell Betsy not to burn my eggs. I had to work an extra security shift last night. Somebody called in sick, and I'm the junior man. Shit rolls downhill." Monk gave Victor the once over, wincing at the ill-fitting formality of the little man's outfit. In the year he'd been working as a guard at the track, he'd never seen the bum in anything but a dirty tee shirt and khaki pants covered with so many stains they looked like a painter's palette. "Victor must be going to a wedding."

"Testify…I say…I'm an important witness, except I don't know nothing. Nothing…I say…nothing. But the prosecutor guy bought me this at Goodwill. He said the grand jury would listen better if I was dressed up. There's a few of us old hardboots got the lucky call to go."

"I thought you didn't know anything," said Monk.

"I say…I know I got a new suit of clothes, and you don't."

Charlie sat a coffee cup in front of Monk and gave him a liberal pour of bourbon into the dark liquid. Monk added a spoon of sugar and stirred vigorously. Gazing around the cavernous room at the empty tables, last night's dirty glasses and beer bottles stacked high waiting for Charlie to get his lazy ass in gear, the unswept floor littered with cigarette butts and sawdust, the corpses of flies dotting the mirror, depressed Monk. He dropped his eyes and stared into the coffee cup to avoid signs of disease and chaos but couldn't ignore the hint of stale beer and Old Spice wafting from Victor. The scenery could have perfectly described Monk's attitude on life.

"Where's my food, goddamnit."

"It's coming," Charlie said. "What's eating you so early in the morning."

"I think Red Harvey's dead."

"No shit. I hadn't seen him in here drinking for a couple of weeks, but he was hitting it pretty hard after his wife run off. Did his liver give out?"

Charlie shivered as he spoke, and Monk remembered what his grandma always told him. That kind of jolt up your backbone means someone just walked over a grave.

"I say…drinkin'll get us all…I say."

"He didn't die from booze. Someone either beat the shit out of him or hit him with a car. They found him in an alley behind Freddie's. That's what they think, anyway. The detective never said which. I have to go identify the body."

"Then you'll need some more of this."

"I told Red the other day that the whiskey at Freddie's was poison," said Victor.

Charlie set a shot of Jim Beam in front of Monk and looked at Victor sideways.

"It's all poison. That's why you losers drink it and why I make a profit."

"Was it an accident?" asked Victor.

"Cops don't know and don't seem to much care. What's one more dead bum to them. Although, I doubt getting beat to death would classify as an accident. Weren't you listening to what I just said?" Monk asked.

Shaking his head, Charlie walked toward the kitchen to check on Monk's breakfast. The hand-rolled cigarette between Victor's beak-like lips bounced up and down like a fishing bobber on a windy lake as he began to speak. Monk had never seen the parrot-looking face without a smoke poking out of it.

"I say…you think someone might of killed Red?"

"He could be pretty annoying."

"Yeah, but you don't kill a guy 'cause he irritates you…I say."

"No, or you'd be dead right now. What other reason could there be to kill Red Harvey?"

"Yeah, but that's discouraging…I say… getting killed for being annoying."

The double doors at the end of the bar swung open. Charlie reappeared followed by the short order cook Betsy. She carried Monk's breakfast plate in both hands like an offering to a god. At least Monk wished that to be the case. The smell of bacon and slightly burned toast along with the whiskey buoyed his spirits.

"Here comes the most beautiful woman I know," he said.

"Then you know very few women," Betsy replied.

She's young, Monk thought, maybe early twenties, but not stupid. She had street smarts and white straight teeth. She smiled a lot, and he was very fond of her teeth. Monk couldn't stand a woman with false or crooked or missing teeth. He wasn't sure why but felt like it must have had something to do with all the old women that joined his mother for her Bible group. They all had false teeth that fit poorly, clacking when they spoke, and they always smiled at him like they knew something he didn't. He learned to hate them for that, and eventually hate the whole idea of religion, conning poor people out of dollar bills they had saved from money they couldn't spare. She told him that the preachers and revival meetings passing through their hometown of Royston, Georgia, was a service performed by those good men of God to give the hopeless hope. Life had taught Monk that giving hope to some people is an impossible task as well as an excuse to steal from them.

Betsy set the hot plate in front of him and brushed a lock of red hair off her sweating forehead. With her other hand, she reached into her apron pocket and handed him a fork.

"I didn't burn your eggs today. Maybe you'll leave a tip for a change, tight ass."

They both laughed and she held his eyes with her own beautiful green ones for an instant.

"How about I come back when your shift's over and we go for a ride in my truck."

"I've done that already. It didn't work out well. How about you dry out, get a real job, and I'll consider it."

"I say…"

"Don't say it, Victor. Instead, tell me what the grand jury thinks you know," Monk said.

"I say…can't right now. It's a secret."

He drank off the shot of bourbon Charley had poured earlier and shook the glass indicating a refill. Victor squirmed on the barstool to face him. The little man's skin had taken on a smoky gray color and his eyes looked slightly jaundiced. Monk glanced at the mirror over the bar making sure his face wasn't showing too many signs of liver damage. He figured himself about ten years younger than Victor. Maybe he'd quit drinking someday. Maybe he would dry out for Betsy. Maybe hell would freeze over, and the world would be at peace. He shook his head and waved a hand disgustedly at the DA's improbable witness.

Headline: Man of Questionable Character Needs Direction in Life

Monk laughed out loud as he entered the Louisville municipal government building, so loud that a crowd of lawyers and clerks and one security guard stopped what they were doing to stare. Half drunk and half asleep, disheveled, and dragging his bad leg slightly, he must have seemed like a deranged vagrant to most of them. Still, he couldn't help himself. The idea that he might have been God's servant was almost as ludicrous as the idea that Jesus would send any monk to fight a war. Yet, his service in Vietnam had branded him with the label of Monk. Irony abounded in his life. Maybe, life itself was ironic. Evidently, people needed stories to give them hope and, the more outrageous the story, the greater the sense of hope it created. He walked to the reception desk and lit a cigarette while the security guard answered a phone call. By the time the guard hung up the phone, Monk's patience, along with his cigarette, was at its end.

"Help you?"

"Yeah, this month if possible."

"Sir, are you drunk."

"No, not yet. The police sent me down here to look at a dead body."

"There's a dead body here?"

Monk's breakfast of Beam and bacon had worn thin. His mouth was full of cotton and his brain was full of thumb tacks. He looked at the name on the card Detective Phelps had given him.

"Isn't Dr. Greathouse here?"

The guard at the information desk chuckled. He pointed to a sign hanging by the elevators slightly behind and across the shiny checkered tile floor. People milled past, shoes clacking like snare drums. The scents of Aqua Velva, English leather, burnt coffee, and hair spray twisted around in Monk's nose and stirred the beginnings of nausea in his whiskey and grease laden stomach. Red Harvey being dead had turned into another pain-in-the-ass. The little prick was becoming just as annoying dead as alive.

"Mister, we got lawyers, politicians, clerks, judges, bailiffs, cops, city planners, secretaries, and janitors in this building. Some of them probably should be dead and the dead probably do more work than most of them. But, if you want to see Doc Greathouse you'll have to go to 810 Barrett Street. They moved the coroner's office there."

"Just my luck. Work all night and get a tour of the city all fucking day."

"It's not that far."

The guard tore a sheet of paper from a clipboard, turned it over to the blank side and drew a simple map plotting a line of travel. Monk thanked the man and started to leave. There had never been a way for him to explain the feeling that next overwhelmed him. He first began getting the warm flush and the tingle it produced on the back of his neck in Vietnam. Then blood roared through his veins with a whooshing sound behind both eardrums and ended in a knot of pressure so tight he expected the back of his head to blow out. Never, in all the times the feeling happened, did there appear any reason for it. Always, a reason became clear seconds later and often saved his life. He would notice the glint of metal in a windowpane that morphed into a gun barrel, hear rustling of trash in a shadowed Saigon alley that signaled a VC trailing him, or taste cordite in the air before an explosion.

Glancing around the lobby of the municipal building quickly, he saw only people lost in the trivia of their own lives. No one seemed aware of his existence, or if they did, indicated any interest whatsoever. Was he beginning to have those flashbacks so many veterans spoke about? Did the ghosts of his past create anxiety attacks for the present? Nothing was out of place. Nothing threatened him except memory. Then, as he reached the door leading outside to Broadway and his truck, the need to find significance in his instincts pulled him around one last time just as an elevator door opened.

Into the lobby walked Elvie Coomer, a well-known bookie and distrusted by every horseman at the racetrack. Beside him, a distinguished man in a dark suit gestured to still another man behind them both who remained out of hearing range. The man next to Elvie appeared prematurely gray. Maybe mid-forties and well-manicured, he held himself aloof from his surroundings and looked at Elvie with disdain, as if he were forced to speak with an IRS agent or a traffic cop. Monk had no idea who the man was but couldn't help wonder why any important and wealthy looking gentleman might need to converse with a slime ball like Elvie.

On the other hand, the broad-shouldered fellow standing a few feet away from them both was easy to size up. Monk had run into his kind several times in the military, dead eyes and a constant vicious smirk, his blond hair trimmed close. The man's large hands were folded into each other directly in front of his waist and his legs balanced his body in an alert stance. This was the kind of guy who took out the trash for the other one, the kind of guy that didn't mind hurting people. Elvie feared them both. The squat little troll shifted his eyes off the one man to the bigger more dangerous looking one several times during a brief, whispered conversation. Even though something was now out of place and Monk felt relieved because it meant his instincts were still intact, he had no idea why Elvie might be in this building. And certainly whatever the reason was, it didn't relate to his search for the coroner. Tucking the anomaly away in the back of his mind, he walked into the languid Louisville morning and immediately began to sweat out the remnants of Mr. Jim Beam.

Headline: Finding the Dead Isn't Always Easy

After twenty minutes of twists and turns in his old Chevy pickup truck around the streets on his list, streets with revolutionary names like Liberty, Lexington, Payne, and Spring and after thinking he found the right one, which turned out to be Baxter instead of Barret, Monk slammed on his brakes. They squealed like an injured dog—a sure sound that he needed new brake pads. He had just toured an older part of Louisville full of rundown warehouses, factories, rusted train tracks, and a slaughterhouse that stank like rotten hog flesh. Back at the corner of Payne and Spring, he checked his pocket watch and found morning had wasted away into an approaching lunch time. Monk still had not been to sleep. What saved him from nodding off behind the steering wheel was the discovery that the intersection was home to a long, one-story building made from concrete blocks and painted several shades of neon reds, greens, and blues. On one wall, some would-be calligrapher had scrawled *Willinger's Tavern*. The letters were scribbled as if the painter had also been a good customer. Here, he refreshed his waning spirit with three quick, cold Pabst Blue Ribbon beers served by a dumpy matron whose ill-fitting false teeth clacked, jolting his nerves like intermittent electric shocks, as she redirected his path to the coroner's office.

It was close to noon when Monk stumbled upon his journey's end. Lighting a Lucky Strike, he inhaled the bluish smoke deeply, thankful for the invigorating poison as he parked his vehicle in the assigned lot. The security guard took a minute to marvel at the wisdom of mediocre bureaucrats. 810 Barret was flanked on one side by a hospital and on the other a church. The city planners had chosen to build the new morgue between a place where incompetent medical care could kill people and visionaries of some imaginary kingdom could send them off. The coroner collected and packaged them for the trip. It made perfect sense, an assembly line for souls and fit perfectly into Monk's ironic world vision. The building itself, in keeping with the apathetic tone of the neighborhood, had been built with rust-colored bricks interjected with hermetically sealed windows at even intervals along the front. It rose three stories to a flat roof like a sterile and empty flower box resting on the front porch of Hell. The windows were tinted and reflected the bright June sunlight back onto the asphalt parking lot making the bottom of Monk's feet burn through the rubber soles of his black Converse sneakers. It could have been any one of a thousand admin buildings in a thousand cities and housed the city sewage treatment plant as easily as the morgue.

As he entered the building through the revolving glass door, the whishing sound and the burst of cold wind from the air-conditioned lobby generated a violent shiver along his spinal chord. He remembered the proverb that flashed through his mind at J.C.'s a few hours earlier that his grandma Johnson used to tell him as a child. "Whenever you shiver like that it means someone has walked over a grave." Monk had no idea whose grave had just been violated, or why it crossed his mind twice in the same morning. All he knew was that he wanted to be someplace, anyplace, else, and he silently cursed Detective Phelps for forcing this responsibility on him. Most of all, he hated Red Harvey for dying.

The foyer stood empty and smelled metallic, like the inside of a welding shop. Checking his pocket watch, he saw it was now twelve-fifteen. Late and past his bedtime when he worked night shifts, but time only matters really if you're in prison. He guessed the clerks and receptionists had gone to lunch. Still, the building felt creepy, as if he'd entered the setting for some zombies in a movie, and they were about to rush at him from behind the several doors leading off into different dark directions. Following the signs on the wall into the hallway leading to the morgue, he found himself standing in an area colder even than the one he left. In the room itself, low fluorescent lighting cast a shadow-like form across a stainless-steel necropsy table. It appeared to Monk as if the wraith who occupied that space was eating a sandwich.

"Hello," said Monk, as more of a question than a greeting. "Dr. Greathouse?"

"Nope. He's gone to lunch. He's the only one in the coroner's office who can afford to eat out."

The man rose from the table and took two steps toward Monk. With a half-eaten sandwich in his left hand, the man extended his right. Monk hesitated. Without knowing where that hand had been, he had no desire to touch it. On top of that, the guy looked like an anorexic tax accountant. His thick, black rimmed glasses rested crookedly on the bridge of his aquiline nose. His skin, the color of bleached flour, stretched so tightly across his face Monk got the impression his huge eyes might pop out at any given moment. The man wore a pencil-thin black tie over a white shirt that seemed beige in comparison to his skin. He took another bite of the sandwich as Monk gripped his hand, which was cold and dry. Chewing, the man looked his visitor over and spoke with a full mouth.

"Bologna's all I can afford on a deputy coroner's salary. Don't worry about being uncomfortable. Everyone is the first time. Smell bothering you?"

"No," Monk lied, "I work on a racetrack full of horse shit and drunks that puke and piss themselves on a regular basis." The stench of death had its own peculiar odor, which he knew and understood, but in this building, it was mixed in a cloud of several chemicals. It was a new and unsettling odor.

"Well, it's not bad in here now anyway. I only got the one body in the freezer and nothing open. My name's Jerome. Dr. Greathouse left me in charge. You here to see the little red headed fellow who's mostly bald and missing an ear."

Monk began to sweat even in the cold. Why can't people shut up unless you ask them for information, especially ghouls in high-water pants with mustard on their ties.

"A cop named Phelps sent me down here to ID that body. Let's get it over with."

"You wouldn't know how he lost that ear, would you?" asked Jerome as he shuffled over to a wall of stainless-steel doors and opened one. "I'm just kind of curious."

"I know exactly how he lost it. It got bit off in a bar fight over by the racetrack when he got caught cheating in a poker game."

In the strained silence that followed, Monk focused on identifying the new smells. The strongest one that had superseded the perfume of death was isopropyl alcohol, then Betadine solution, and formaldehyde, combined into the sterile stink of nothingness that seemed to ooze from Jerome's pores. The closer Monk got to the deputy coroner the more the bile rose in his throat. He rushed to a sink and let the stench do its work. Up came his breakfast eggs and his lunch time beers. The vomiting purified and calmed him and the emptiness in his stomach brought relief.

"Jesus," yelled Jerome, "now I got a mess…"

"No you don't. It's all in the sink. Just turn on the fucking water. Come on, let's get this over with."

Sliding a long tray out of the wall, Jerome turned down a white sheet to expose Red Harvey's corpse. What should have raised Monk's conscience to a serious level of pity didn't. He felt only numb. Gazing around the room at the sterilized objects that recently held pieces of humans, the centrifuge, the scales, the cadaver mover, autopsy sinks, and necropsy tables, and then back to the bruised and battered shell, he couldn't muster any grief for Red Harvey, card cheat, fake preacher, lover of horses, and drunk. Even when he realized the sad truth that Red had no family or friends, Monk found no reservoir of grief that he might drink from. What overwhelmed him and suffocated his soul was the only emotion he could muster. Fear. Fear, along with the knowledge that this was most certainly to be his own fate one day, a lonely death. Everyone died alone.

"That's Red Harvey. But, those sure don't look like tire marks on his chest," said Monk.

"Tire marks?"

"Yeah, Phelps said old Red got smacked by a car."

"Only if the car was the shape and size of a Louisville Slugger. Phelps always thinks a beat-up body lying in the street is a hit and run victim. It makes his life easier because he can turn the case over to someone else."

"He said he was on the scene."

"So was I. See, everybody forgets that about us. The coroner's office has been around since 1780. Course, I haven't been here that long." The deputy coroner let loose a high-pitched giggle that sounded like a Louisiana swamp nutria on a hot date. "We go out to every dead body. We don't wait for it to come to us. I'm telling you, this guy made someone really angry, and that someone beat him up."

"Mad enough for murder?" Like Monk had mentioned to Victor earlier that morning, Red Harvey could be annoying, but irritation doesn't usually lead to murder.

"That's what I thought at first, two drunks in a bad fight, and I told Phelps that when he got to the alley where the corpse was. But look at this." Jerome twisted the neck from left to right with both hands and then lifted what was left of Red's ear to expose a round, red hole about the size of a dime, maybe slightly smaller. "I seen lots of these. I did a tour as a medic in 'Nam eight years ago before the shit really hit the fan bad. That's a small caliber bullet hole. Doc Greathouse X-rayed the skull and you can see where the lead rattled around the skull and came to rest in the brain. He hasn't dug it out yet, but he will after lunch. Probably a .22, I'd guess."

"Somebody beat him up, *then* shot him."

"There were two assailants. This didn't happen simultaneously. Whoever did this wanted to make sure the old boy was truly dead. This seems professional to me. Not like somebody got mad and beat him up in a fight, and then had enough presence of mind to think maybe he better shoot him also. I'm thinking there were two different agendas at work here by two different people. The beating didn't kill him. At the same time that idea also seems ridiculous. Who'd hire a hit man for an old bum like this? Is Harvey his last name?"

"I don't know. I got no idea what his last name was, or even if he had one."

As Jerome started to zip the bag over Red Harvey for the last time ever, Monk notice some ink on the corpse jut below the left shoulder and across the bicep, a tattoo. SEMPER FI 1/9 underneath that, eight letters-DI BO CHET.

"That's kind of sad, especially since you seem to be his only friend," said Jerome.

"One of the many things in life that are,"

Monk intended these last words on the way out of the morgue to be an off-handed, matter-of-fact statement on the condition of the world. Nothing personal. Something for Jerome to mull over with his bologna sandwich. Consequently, he was shocked when his eyes got wet and his legs felt like rubber as he walked to his pickup truck in the blanched afternoon sunlight. So, old Red Harvey was a Vietnam vet, a member of the famed 1st Battalion, 9th Marine Regiment, Di Bo Chet, Vietnamese for "The Walking Dead" and reason enough to consider that the murder victim had earned some justice. You don't go through the stuff this outfit did in 'Nam without gaining a whole lot of respect. The questions were building in Monk's mind. Who killed this fellow vet and why? It must have been more than a bar fight, and Red Harvey's death deserved closure, if for no other reason than that tattoo on his arm.

Headline: Research Proves Long Naps May Be Unhealthy

He strolled along the river around the Bason shipyard alone with his rain poncho draped over his uniform and the hood pulled over his helmet. It was foggy, but he could still recognize Saigon. He got into the habit of bringing food scraps along and throwing them to the starving, mangy dogs along the docks and alleyways he patrolled on MP duty. These were the lucky dogs that hadn't found their way into a stew pot. Soon, a pack of regulars trailed behind him, warning him of approaching footsteps or strange smells with their snarling whispers. A couple of drunken sailors on shore leave were pissing on a lamp post when he appeared out of the river mist.

"Jesus," one said.

"Not Jesus," said the other. "He looks like that monk fellow that had all them dogs following him all the time, that saint guy with my cousin's name. Saint Frank, I think."

By the time he escorted them all the way back to lockup for the night so they wouldn't get killed by some VC chick posing as a hooker, they had forgotten the name, but "arrested by the Monk" stuck. As is the way with all war myths, stories traveled quickly of a former Benedictine cleric visited in his cloistered cell by a vision of Jesus that sent him on this mission. The Holy Spirit gave him almost superhuman power and protection from evil. His stare could paralyze you while he read your mind. The spirits of dead Buddhist VC who had crossed his path became the dogs that served him as karmic retribution for trying to kill him. The mention of the name brought respect. Monk sounded more ominous in the presence of a bitter, skinny, silent kid from Royston, Georgia than Harold.

An air conditioner thumped as the compressor kicked on in the Paddock Tavern next door to his sleeping room. His room was stuffy and smelled of decaying earth, bug spray, and stale beer. The sheets were soaked with sweat. This picture in his mind came and went often, like a video tape on a recurring loop. It happened at that time when you are never sure whether you're awake or asleep, whether the images in your mind were memories or dreams. Years away from a war, and he was still there.

When Monk awoke fully and sat up in bed the sweat on his back vaporized, replaced by a sudden chill. He grabbed his cigarettes from the nightstand, lit one with his old Zippo, and picked up his pocket watch. It was 6:45PM. He had napped for almost six hours since returning from the morgue and might as well plan for a night out. There was no way he would fall asleep again before the wee hours of tomorrow morning. Working the night shift had put his sleeping habits in an uproar even when he had a day off, as if sleep came easy anyway. He needed a shower and several drinks to dissipate the rage rising from an unknown place in his brain. Monk hated this darkness that came over him without warning or cause every time he awoke from one of his half dreams. The only thing that limited it was a propitiatory numbness that would send it scurrying back underneath the mental rock it crawled out from under. His self-awareness over the last few years had developed enough to recognize his flawed lifestyle. But being aware of a broken engine doesn't fix it. Maybe he needed a woman to take the edge off, to straighten him out, and in the last couple of weeks a particular one had dominated his thoughts.

After a quick shower and shave in the cramped communal bathroom down the hallway, Monk searched through his cheap wooden dresser for something appropriate to wear. If he had any obsessions, this was one, certainly. Each drawer contained only certain items of clothing and each item had been folded according to the military order he learned in the Army. It literally drove him crazy to find a sock stuck to a pair of briefs or anything else he'd missed during laundry at the coin-operated laundromat on Fourth Street next to Becker & Durski's Turf Supplies. Socks were paired and placed in the top drawer only, briefs in the second, tee-shirts in the third. The bottom drawer was stacked with three pairs of neatly creased Levi's. His guard uniforms, two shirts with buttons and collars and a pair of dress trousers he owned along with one gray suit hung perfectly pressed and in order from left to right on a makeshift metal rack against the wall at the foot of his bed. In this way, Monk controlled his environment of cheap beige dry wall, scratched up furniture, and urine-colored shag carpet. At the same time, he created a sense of order from the chaotic world of memories and possibilities in his mind. He wasn't sure when the need to organize his laundry began but remembered doing it ever since he was discharged in '71.

Settling on a black silk shirt covered in huge yellow flowers bought in Okinawa and an almost new pair of jeans, he dressed quickly and still sweating from the shower, stepped next door to the Paddock. Here in the nearly deserted barroom, Monk swallowed a shot of Jim Beam and a foaming draft Pabst without speaking to the bartender. A man named Willard and who seemed to be slightly off kilter in some indiscernible way had started the evening shift. They all knew Monk's drinking habits, and Willard simply raked the money from the bar top. Both men nodded simultaneously.

Monk had thought no more of Red Harvey since the trip to the morgue. Now, fully awake, the image of the little man's corpse forced its way back into his consciousness. He couldn't come to terms with the idea that someone had hated the little hardboot badly enough to beat him to death or that Red had enough money in his pocket to make a robbery worthwhile. All that left was a professional hit, and that scenario made less sense than the other two. Red Harvey was the least important person Monk knew; certainly nothing in Red's life would generate a contract killing. Would it?

The nagging in his mind became an itch as he slid from the bar stool. The itch became a throb by the time he reached the door. Finally, he spun around, returned to the bar and bought a half-pint of Beam, which he opened immediately after unlocking his pickup truck. One big swig eased the bass drum in his brain. What had been a living person yesterday became a shadow, a form without substance, like many others in Monk's past. He tossed the bottle into the glove box for later before driving three blocks to J.C's and thought no more of Red Harvey.

Headline: Life Is Not an Art, But Art Can Be Life

If Monk had been a painter, he would have stopped in his tracks, put up an easel and gone to work. The familiar Wurlitzer jukebox flashed red and green neon light in one corner. Pale blue cigarette smoke drifted across the tables and up into the dim glow of the lamps above the bar. A Miller beer sign had just enough bulbs burned out so all that lit up was *High Life*. Charlie had been joined behind the bar by Betsy, who worked fast enough mixing drinks that her cheeks were flushed. She greeted Monk with a smile, and he felt a rush of warmth in the air-conditioned room. At least thirty people or so he recognized from the track lined the bar and filled the chairs around the scattered tables. Charlie's two evening waitresses slung pitchers of beer in varying directions and raked dollar bills into the pockets of their stained aprons. Neither was much to look at. One was young and chubby with enough facial hair above her lip to qualify as a moustache. The other listed left when she walked as if she might fall from the tray on her arm. She must have been at least fifty with huge, black-rimmed glasses and skin the consistency and color of wallpaper paste. But people who traveled the racing circuit knew what it meant to work hard and when they got well-oiled with booze, they tipped heavy. Appearance didn't matter much as long as the drinks kept coming. Not only that, but Monk knew that each of these women would receive at least a dozen marriage proposals before the bar closed.

Yes, the scene before him would have been a masterpiece on canvas that he could call *Paradise*. It was all in front of him, everything he needed to make him feel whole, at least temporarily. Drinks were cheap and the crowd, already boisterous. No one judged him in here, and he judged no one back. Sure, occasionally someone lost his temper over an insult to a lady friend, an accusation of a fixed race or a bad ride, and bottles got thrown along with a few punches. But even the violence was understood to be part of life. Monk remembered when Charlie had the building sided with metal strips a few months ago. He just covered over most of the windows so they wouldn't have to be replaced every time some drunk threw a chair or another drunk through one. Every night during the summer race season, the same gang drowned away the monotonous routine of the day. J.C's was just the place Monk was looking for, a sanctuary away from the morgue, the nagging questions surrounding Red's demise, and from the misery of Monk's own bad memories. He felt anger rise again and waved at Rachel, the younger waitress, to bring him a beer.

"You want a shot of tequila, Dirty Harry?" Angel Martinez rose from his chair as he asked the question. Like the five other people sitting around the table just inside the door, Angel was a friendly acquaintance. He rode races, but not very well. The only thing that got him a lot of mounts was his naturally light weight. Angel had never weighed over a hundred and ten pounds in his life. Still, Monk respected his courage. The willingness to do what needed to be done no matter how afraid you might be to do it defined a man as far as Monk was concerned, a way to measure a person's true worth that he learned during the war. This son-of-a-bitch Angel would get on anything with four legs, no matter how crippled, or how rank, and ride the best race he could. He would take the inside rail turning for home or stick and drive up behind a wall of horses on a crippled horse that could break down any second. His face was round and deeply tanned. A long scar ran across his left cheek from below the eye to the bottom of his sideburn.

Like always, Doc Tandini had stopped at J.C's on his way home from the track for one drink and was now half-drunk, showing no sign of slowing down. The veterinarian sometimes gave Monk a tip on a horse that Doc had juiced up, and usually Monk bet a few bucks on the horse if he was off security guard duty. Doc had a way of getting the chemical best out of an athlete without getting caught by the stewards.

It wasn't a sure thing, nothing really ever was in horse racing or life. But the horses usually ran pretty solid races. He was very popular with trainers. Barbara Miller, a freelance pony girl that made extra money galloping horses during training hours sat beside Doc. She and Doc were frequent barhopping partners. Barb's rough, growling voice, close-cropped hair, and "fuck you" attitude intimidated any drunken cowboys that didn't know how tough she was going in and saw her as an easy mark, not to mention the fact she was almost six feet tall and could lift a bale of hay over her head with one hand. Susie and Ron Jackson rounded out the table. They were a husband-and-wife training team that had raced bush league tracks since before Monk was old enough to read a Racing Form. They were hardboots, lifetime race trackers who eked a living out of traveling the circuit with a few cheap claiming horses, and therefore on his list of good people.

"Sure Angel but make it bourbon. I don't want any nasty ass bar tequila."

"You're drinking pretty heavy, sweetie. Trouble?" asked Barb.

"Are you kidding? Any man that gets a look at those two, big, beautiful, blue eyes is the one in trouble." Monk joked, slightly embarrassed that his expression gave away his attitude so easily. What was taking Angel so long with his bourbon?

"Any man who gets a look at those two big, beautiful…" Ron started to add his perspective to the conversation, but Susie smacked him playfully, and Ron, being a wise married man, shut up.

"It doesn't have to be trouble," Doc said, "Any of us who've been knocking around these damn racetracks for very long has got plenty to drink about. All that scratching and fighting to make a living, meanwhile the big stables run one expensive horse after another down your throats… it's tough. It gets to you."

"First of all, Monk's a sort-of-cop and God damn it, you're a vet. What the hell would either of you know about trying to compete with big outfits? He rousts winos from the tack rooms and hands out parking tickets. You just drive around in your new Cadillac and shoot up lame horses with drugs to keep them going and collect your money," said Ron, as he lit a cigarette.

"You forgot one thing, asshole."

"What?"

"When you guys don't win races, I have a hell of time getting my money."

Monk pulled up a chair and sat down. He would spend a few minutes swapping bullshit stories before approaching Betsy at the bar. The best way to get laid was pretend you didn't want to get laid. Angel came back from the bar, set the shot of bourbon down, and without sitting himself, walked over to one of the pool tables. Two other riders and a trainer named Gabe McKay wanted him to join their game of nine ball and Angel never turned down an offer to gamble on a pool game.

Tuning out the mindless hum of his friends' voices, Monk looked at the various dead deer and fish mounted on the wall above the pool tables. Wouldn't it be nice if people would learn to hang pictures instead of dead animals on the wall? Unless you had lived for a time in the proximity of death, it was hard to understand the true value of life. Of course, if you lived with death long enough, if it became a daily occurrence, then at some point life had no value at all. It was an emotional paradox. Monk was slowly coming to realize that surviving had a lot to do with balance, being able to walk the tight rope between too much and too little. One misstep off either side and down you went.

"A penny for your thoughts," said Barbara.

Monk turned around and noticed a concerned expression of her face. He knew her to be the sort of person, besides being tough as nails, who would also pick up a baby bird that had fallen from the nest and try to nurse it long enough for it to fly away. He believed her question was sincere.

“I had to identify a body today at the morgue.”

“A body? Shit, who died.”

“Remember the guy that used to preach on the backside when he was drunk and hot walk horses. He had part of his ear missing. Yeah, well, somebody murdered him two days ago.”

Barbara pounded her glass on the table like a judge calling traffic court to order. Ron, Susie, and Doc looked up simultaneously with startled frowns.

“What the…,” said Doc.

“Somebody murdered old Red Harvey.”

“Red Harvey? He was harmless, a little crazy and a cheater at cards, but harmless.” Susie seemed frightened as she spoke, as if the knowledge that a soul like Red could fall victim to a murderer put her in personal jeopardy.

“How did it happen?” Ron asked.

“Somebody beat the hell out of him so it looked like a bar fight and then somebody put a bullet in his brain execution style,” Monk said. “It’s a very weird crime committed by probably two different guys with a gun according to this scarecrow looking fellow at the morgue.”

“Or maybe, somebody worked him over for information *before* they killed him.”

Doc’s statement gave everyone at the table pause, including Monk. He had been a military policeman and been good at it. Yet, he had become so jaded and cynical, possibly apathetic, that the idea of Red being tortured for information never crossed his mind. Red had nothing anybody wanted. It didn’t make sense.

“What kind of info would Red Harvey have that would be worth torture and murder for?” asked Barbara. Ron nodded, agreeing with her question.

"I'm not saying he did, but rumor has it he was one of several trackers scheduled to appear before a grand jury called to investigate a gambling ring," Doc answered.

"Yeah, yeah, we hear stories about gambling conspiracies at every track we go to. Somebody's always got a way to rig races. Somebody's always got a sure thing. That's why we're all rich," said Ron, and the whole table erupted in spontaneous laughter.

"Racing stewards, prosecutors, grand juries, bureaucrats have to keep busy. They need to justify their existence in some way. No one could fix a race or races to where enough money was involved on an impossible sure thing to go around murdering people. Besides, saying something's going on doesn't mean you can prove it anyway," Susie said.

"No, you're right," said Doc, beginning to raise the intensity and tone of his voice. "On the other hand, what I'm hearing is that somebody bred a whole bunch of ringers. You put a ringer in the right race and it's as close to a lock as you can get in this business. It'll outclass and outrun everything in the field. A whole stable full of them could make you a fortune."

"There's no way to beat the tattoo system. They got an ID on every racehorse in the country and once those numbers are inked in under a horse's lip, you might as well forget changing them." Ron was right. Everyone at the table knew it. "Besides, even if Doc's idea proved correct, it doesn't make sense that a drunk like Red would be involved in it. That'd be like making a homeless guy a real estate broker in Beverly Hills."

"Then you tell me why he got a subpoena from the prosecutor's office." An indignant Doc Tandini spoke and raised an empty glass and shook it at Betsy. She smiled at Monk and began to mix another scotch and soda.

"Maybe there's a rash of old hardboot drunks pissing on fire hydrants around the track. We'll call it the urination conspiracy for Doc's benefit."

Barb said and rolled her eyes. On the conversation went, each person expressing some sort of remembrance in honor of Red Harvey. As the drinks flowed more freely, the old boy's status grew exponentially. He saved a baby from a burning building, carried his last cup of water to a thirsty nun, gave someone the shirt off his back, donated kidneys and lungs, hearts and livers to the sick, bathed lepers and, if not for his lust for women, might have become pope.

Even though no one knew Red more than enough to say hello or give him five bucks to cool out a horse, he was part of their extended family by virtue of the way he lived. The conversation became a memorial service of hyperbole until it diffused into an even drone in Monk's mind. The words were indistinguishable from the blue cigarette smoke twisting around the ceiling fans or the rattle of ice cubes and the clatter of billiard balls. With each shot of bourbon, Betsy's presence behind the bar became more urgent and more formidable until it almost filled the room, melting everyone else into her energy. Was she someone who could satisfy more than lust, fill some vague hunger Monk couldn't even recognize for more than a day? Did a single person exist in the whole universe that could erase his nightmares and make him feel like more than a broken machine.

Headline: Man Goes Buggy for Love

The night was so clear and the moon so close, Monk could almost see himself reflected in its surface. He wanted Betsy alone with him, and he wanted the world quiet. Having driven her to a small beach on the cut bank of the Ohio River after her shift at J. C.'s ended, both desires were accomplished. Now, he didn't know what he should do. The water flowed beneath him softly and the splash of the current playing off the different sized stones along the shoreline sounded like xylophones tinkling through some jazz song, writing the melody new with each thrust of forward motion. Nocturnal insects clicked and clacked in rhythm and the world seem so serene that Monk barely noticed the sweltering blanket woven of heat and humidity that hugged them both.

If he could just lay on the blanket with her, keep looking at the stars, sip his half pint of bourbon, and not remember anything, the world would be forever in his control. He wanted a few hours of slow time, a brief period when his mind didn't race with memories and possibilities, possibilities and memories. The roar and crash of thoughts deposited images of Red's corpse mixed with the faces of the war dead on his consciousness. For God's sake, was it too much to ask for some sort of peace, even a temporary sort of peace? Then, a whiff of fish rotting and summer souring the river mixed with the scent of honeysuckle and green hay around them. His sense of smell became an open conduit between where he was and where he had already been.

The last woman Monk cared anything about had left him quickly and painfully wounded, not like the shrapnel and bullet wounds he received in Vietnam. Those tore his flesh from the outside in. The woman he had married upon returning from Vietnam, injured him from the inside out. His thoughts drifted toward other women he had slept with since her, the whore in Old Louisville who whispered any name he wanted for extra money when he climaxed and the two sisters in Bullitt County. Their brother made the best moonshine he'd ever tasted. The Catholic married woman during Mardi Gras who let him do anything he wanted except penetrate her vagina because she refused to be unfaithful to her husband, did she count? There were others too, but he could barely remember faces let alone names. Sex was like shaking hands, just a way to say hello. He thanked his generation for that casual lack of responsibility. As far as sex, Monk had always been a hippie.

Being with someone didn't make you part of someone though. When Monk left these other women, he left them entirely. They were shadows in a fog with human forms. They were meaningless except as receptacles for his physical needs. He always felt bad after because of this, and yet, couldn't stop himself from repeating his actions at every opportunity. The distance between being with someone and being part of someone was a buffer zone that allowed him to function without risk or pain. He knew it, and he needed it. Now there was confusion swirling beneath this buffer zone in his mind. Like an undertow in the river he sat watching, it pulled and tugged him in a dangerous direction. Here was a woman he very much wanted to be inside of, but also one he wanted inside of him. He felt her warmth, not just next to him on the blanket, but all the way through his body. The myth of the angry, lonely, unstable, drunken, Vietnam veteran, the illusion that protected his emotions from harm, was in danger of being exposed and eliminated by a bar maid he barely knew.

"Aren't the stars great Monk? It's like there's a whole world up there that exists just for us to look at and wonder about."

"I like them because they hang on nothing in a vacuum. They depend on the law of physics and the law of physics never changes. Stars don't have to think about those little unexpected things that happen because there aren't any unexpected occurrences in space."

"What about all those things we studied in high school science class, black holes, super novas?"

Monk rolled over on his stomach and looked at Betsy. His eyes were laughing. He could always feel that rare sensation from the inside, as if the eyeballs were diamonds that saw their own sparkle. She seemed suddenly nervous, twirling a gold hoop hanging from her earlobe and repositioning herself against the cool earth of the cut bank. Gazing across the river, they both saw a tugboat push five barges full of coal into the narrow channel slowly.

"I've got an answer. Suppose all those things you just mentioned weren't surprises. Suppose they happened in harmony with the life and death of each star and everything in the universe moved along exactly like it should with the exception of the things people interfered with on this planet?"

"I never would have figured you to spend time thinking about all this stuff."

"It used to be what I thought about all the time, how things worked, why they worked that way, how beautiful it was to be part of some higher purpose even if I didn't know what that purpose was."

"I'm glad to finally be talking with a man whose brain is above his waist. I just never believed it would have been you. Does that upset you?"

"No, not really. You see me most often when I'm coming off a dead end, all night job, or when I'm plastered on bourbon and can barely put a sentence together. You're one of two people in this world who knows I read books and can articulate an opinion on things. People leave me alone and don't ask me to do much because they think I'm retarded and dangerous. I like that."

They laughed and Monk two lit cigarettes, handing one to her.

"Who's the other one?"

"The other what?"

"The other person who knows you're not crazy."

"The shrink who treats me at the VA hospital over on Zorn Avenue."

"What about your parents?"

"My dad died when I was a kid and my mother is just another Baptist Bible-thumper from Georgia. She's remarried to a preacher. They don't know me, and I'm not interested in getting re-acquainted with them."

Betsy smacked a mosquito from her shoulder. Monk leaned over and kissed her forearm gently. The move astonished him, not because he didn't expect to take that intimate action, but his kiss was so gentle; it was as if he used someone else's lips. He was a military cop who had put down drunken soldiers routinely with his nightstick and once, a VC down with his .45. He had pulled body parts from buildings in Saigon after bombings, and he acted as a semi-literate thug on his minimum wage job. Yet he found himself quiet in Betsy's presence, as if she drew the anger and violence out of him and spun it away till it dissipated like smoke. Monk was not so much hoping to possess this woman as to touch her. She leaned closer and didn't take her arm away from him. Her skin was electric against his cheek.

"My mind used to work better, I think, but not so much now. Now I just feel numb most of the time, like the dentist had given my brain a big shot of Novocain by mistake," said Monk.

"You're not inspiring much confidence in me for a romantic fellow."

"I'm trying to be honest. I like you and you deserve to know where I'm at, although sometimes I'm not so sure of that myself." He sat quietly for a long time.

"I feel the same way. My mother left me on my own when I was fourteen. I spent my formative years living on the streets. It hurt so much to think about, I just tried to quit. But, I've always wondered if I did something to make her go away...say something Monk, anything."

He didn't speak. He reached across with his left hand and touched her left breast through her tee shirt tentatively as if it were the most valuable and fragile work of art he'd ever seen. The uncertainty and slight prodding of his conscience disappeared with that touch in one red rush of blood from his brain to some small area below his waist. Suddenly, he was in love. All processes involved in reasoning drifted away with a slight rustling in his mind, like leaves blowing across a shingled roof. If this was a mistake, then he wanted to be the kind of man who learned from his mistakes.

"Does that bother you?"

"No, it feels good." She kissed him hard and pushed her body down on his. They kept kissing. He ran his hand under her shirt and caressed the nipple with his fingers. She began to breath heavily, then suddenly pulled away.

"I'm on the pill, but I don't know you Monk. I haven't had much luck with men and you seem like two different men to me."

Her upper lip quivered slightly, and Monk knew she was fighting herself. She was afraid and the fear excited her. Brushing a lock of red hair aside, Max ran his tongue up and down her long, soft neck. He watched her green eyes glaze over slightly, then close. He kissed her again. Betsy fell back on the ground. He lifted her shirt and kissed her flat, smooth stomach. This is the most perfect navel that ever existed, thought Monk as he unbuckled her Levis and slowly pulled the zipper down. She no longer held back, moving her hips under the urging of his fingers. He felt her control and his begin to fade, and then, they were together. With one hand, she massaged the back of his neck. With the other, she tugged at his belt buckle till it opened. He reached under her shirt and cradled her breast. Her breathing quickened as she reached into his pants and held his cock. He moaned and then kissed her angrily. She nicked his upper lip with her teeth till it bled slightly.

He bit her nipples, one at a time. The hint of her pain made him warm all over. He smelled the river, the decaying earth, the tobacco and whiskey on them both, all hanging in the viscous air. It was the perfume of her and he loved it. They sweated together. Monk ran his tongue down her chest and belly, licking the sweat from her navel. His breath came in rapid hisses. He took himself out of his pants and entered her, lifting them both off the earthen bed. She wrapped her legs around his waist and he rode her that way in perfect rhythm for several minutes. They met and separated and met again, her muscles tightening the deeper he went inside her. Neither had spoken until Monk said, "I'm coming." As he began to shudder, he felt flesh fall away from bone. He felt her thigh muscles involuntarily quiver, her stomach tighten and release in spasm after spasm. Wave after wave of electricity rolled up and down the length of their bodies. It felt so good it hurt. "Jesus," she screamed. Monk was spent.

"I'm sorry," he said.

"Oh my God don't be, cowboy. You just won first prize at the rodeo."

After it was over, his reasoning and thought returned. He went limp and the desire to be *with* a woman folded into a small box somewhere beneath his consciousness. Monk wanted to take her as a man takes a woman, but if he let his guard down and admitted that he cared for her as a person, he felt like something in him might die. There was no way to perform physically and emotionally at the same time. The war excised that ability. Now, his great attempt at romance ended as the physical urges passed, and he lay on the blanket with his eyes closed, angry at his failure to be more than a man.

Betsy's long hair tumbled over his face and across his mouth. The smell of cigarette smoke and herbal shampoo began to suffocate him.

He wanted a shot of Jim Beam, a line of coke, electro shock therapy, quick death, anything but having another person next to him relying on him for some type of emotional engagement. Monk wasn't scared of much, but he was terrified of letting something control him, and the weight of another body lying on him was more than he could bear. The Kentucky night sky collapsed around him and, like a spent squeezebox, his lungs ran out of air. The more he tried to breathe, the more Betsy's soft whispers in his ear began to sound like fingernails scraping a blackboard. The more she tucked him into her with those wonderful arms, the more his skin burned as if a million insects bit him relentlessly. He bolted upright. Bugs *were* biting.

"Mosquitoes," Monk screamed, "Head for the truck."

Headline: Monk Makes a Friend

In the gray space before dawn, Monk remembered Red. It was Thursday morning. Three mornings had passed since he had left Betsy in a confused state at her apartment above J.C.'s Bar and Grill and one morning since the new track Chaplin held a memorial service for the dead hot walker in the recently renovated and redecorated Horsemen's all-purpose lounge just beyond the clocker's tower at the back gap of the track. Monk had passed two awkward mornings at J.C.'s eating breakfast in silence and avoided hanging out there in the evenings because he felt unsure of how to proceed with Betsy. The love making and her company were both enjoyable and frightening, but he felt neither could be permanent because nothing in life was.

Now, as he finished the night shift and made one last patrol around the barn area, a black dog approached him tentatively. The dog was covered with mange, looked half-starved, and had managed to escape from somewhere dragging its chain behind. Monk knew every dog licensed to be in the barn area and this mutt wasn't one of them. The chain was wrapped around a small fence post, and the mutt struggled to free itself with what little strength it had left. Pity overwhelmed him. This little guy's life had gone from bad to worse. Abused by its owner, it fought for freedom, and the freedom it attained was killing it. Anger rushed up his spine and knotted in a red ball at the back of his neck. If he could have found the dog's owner, Monk would have beat him senseless just on principle.

The older he got the more thought he put into understanding the subtlety of words. The bridge between absolute meaning and bad judgment was built quicker in youth when adrenaline fired fast enough to make his head ache as if he'd swallowed whole bowls of ice cream. For instance, the bridge between guilt and shame in Vietnam allowed him to cross that blurred line between doing what was right and doing what was expected. On certain occasions, he'd participated in interrogation of VC suspects that greatly exceeded the boundaries of the Geneva Convention. His motivation was the embarrassment that arose whenever he refused to join his fellow MP's in their cruel behavior. He couldn't stand the shame of letting them down.

Over the years, those two words began to stand on their own. A connection didn't need to exist. In some cases they could even oppose each other. Where was the shame he should have felt for the way the VC suspects had been treated, the shame that should have been strong enough to override his petty guilt and spur him into standing against his peers?

On this particular morning while freeing the dog from its trap, Monk felt no guilt and no culpability in Red's death. What he felt was an overwhelming surge of shame that was strong enough to moisten his eyes. Red Harvey was murdered by someone for some reason and the old boy didn't deserve it. Yet, no one seemed to care once he had been buried. Even Detective Phelps hadn't come back around to follow up on any leads. Out of sight, out of mind. The detective never bothered making a return call to mention why he thought a bullet was found in Red's brain. If the death was simply a matter of an argument and the other guy had a gun anyway, why not just shoot Red to begin with? A good cop would have been curious enough to find an answer to that question. Monk was ashamed that Red Harvey had called him a friend. So what if that was only in Red's mind? Shouldn't that be respected instead of ignored? Shouldn't someone be an advocate for Red's memory and for some kind of justice? Did justice exist, really? Nothing would bring Red back to life. Nothing would repay his service and sacrifice in an unjust war. Didn't questions like these exist to be answered?

After he removed the chain, the scruffy, little, curly-haired dog followed him away from the mile chute, and the sun began to rise.

Maybe the little fellow knew they were headed toward the track kitchen and food, or maybe its hunger and hope transcended fear. Monk understood that the comfort arising from a presence of purpose could be contagious.

The track kitchen was Monk's last stop before his shift ended, and it looked the same today as it did most days at dawn. The tables along the west wall were crowded with grooms and hotwalkers arguing over who had the best horse in the best stable, drinking coffee, laughing, and throwing their hands in different directions to punctuate their words. Occasionally one of the braver girls would venture an opinion and then promptly be ridiculed for having no balls, and therefore no intellect. Women were still an oddity in the men's club on the backside of mid-western racetracks in the 1970's, and most of the men viewed them as an inferior species of beast to be used when expedient and disregarded at all other times, like the dogs that guarded the feed sheds. Monk thought this was wrong. If you have to spend all morning looking at a groom bent over a horse in the barn, why should it be an ugly old man? He believed that his attitude contributed, in a small way, to cultural progress. It also made him feel enlightened.

Exercise riders sat at the tables in the center of the room. The racetrack was a closed caste system, riders ranked above grooms, who ranked above hotwalkers. The trainers occupied the highest caste because they paid the bills and gave everyone else employment. The jockeys, who ranked between trainers and exercise riders but considered themselves the highest caste because their jobs were the most dangerous, had already left the kitchen and reported to their agents for a schedule of what barns to visit and who to hustle for future race mounts.

Normally, he would have gotten a cup of coffee from Mildred, the chunky, middle-aged cook who fried the eggs and baked the biscuits in the black, post-midnight AM that kept the bowels of the track open and the arteries clogged. But, he passed by with a wave and a shake of the head. Mildred frowned. She always told Monk that he looked exactly like the short detective on the TV series *Beretta* and that he made her really hot. It also got him free coffee. But, Monk knew his square jaw and scarred forehead and crooked nose made his appearance more along the lines of a bad sparring partner for Muhammad Ali. Mildred allowed her hormones to overrule her vision. Besides, he couldn't worry about flirting with her this particular morning, or take much notice of the friendly catcalls that greeted his arrival. He was on a mission. He would buy a sausage and egg biscuit for his new canine friend on the way out.

Victor sat alone in a corner nursing a cup of coffee. His eyes were half shut and he leaned back in his chair till it rested against the wall. The old boy didn't seem to notice Monk's arrival until the guard rattled an empty chair as he pulled it away from the table and sat.

"I say, you don't look so hot, Dirty Harry. Give out too many parking tickets on the night shift?"

"You think you're looking better? I've seen dead men with better color than you."

"I won the daily double yesterday, I say. You know what that means."

"Yeah, it means all your winnings got drank up last night."

"I say, you got it. I say, what you want bothering me so early into my hangover?"

"I want to know what went on with the grand jury."

The chatter in the track kitchen lessened in humanity, replaced by the clang and clatter of dishes and silverware being stacked on the conveyor belt that led to the sink and the two Mexicans covered with sweat and soap suds who scrubbed and rinsed them . Victor gave Monk a sly glance and smiled.

"I say... You're thinking that might have something to do with Red getting whacked, ain't you? I know your type. You see conspiracies everywhere I say...everywhere."

“I’m just curious. Quit worrying about my type and tell me.”

“Curiosity killed the cat.”

Monk took a five dollar bill from his wallet and smoothed it out on the table top. Then, he pushed it toward the scruffy little man on his right.

“This’ll buy you another daily double ticket this afternoon.”

“I say shit…you *are* curious. I’ll take your money, but you won’t get the answers you’re looking for.”

“Let me be the judge of that.”

Victor shoved the bill into his shirt pocket, leaned his chair forward and stuck his face close to Monk’s. His breath, a cross between dead fish and horse piss, stunned the security guard for a second. He shook his head to clear the stench away.

“Seems like the prosecuting attorney here in Louisville got wind of one of your little conspiracies. A rich horse breeder from Lexington, Whitney Landis III, has his eye on the governorship of the great state of Kentucky. Problem is…I say…it takes good planning and a lot *more* money than ole Whitney’s got to run for office.”

“You’re boring me with politics.”

“I say…that’s what I told the prosecutor, Gimme a cigarette.”

“You asked the prosecutor for a smoke?”

“No, I asked you for one. I told him I was bored with his speechifying, already.”

The air in the track kitchen already a grey and blue tint from the cigars, pipes, and cigarettes that had been lit one after another. Monk figured more smoke was going to do little damage to the corrupt air. Besides, maybe a nose full of good smoke would rid him of the stench of Victor. He wondered if the guy passed out drunk on his cot and pissed himself sometime during the night. Monk prayed someone would love him enough to put a round through his brain if he ever turned into that kind of a drunk. He wished it might be Betsy for a moment, but realized she was far too kind-hearted to do the necessary things that life sometimes requires.

Shaking out two Luckies from a half-empty pack, he handed one to Victor and put one between his own thick lips. The lucky Zippo fired the first time. He never went anywhere without it. Monk lit both smokes.

"Now, get on with it," he said with the smoke from his lungs punctuating each word.

"Well, three years ago at the same time Landis starts thinking about politics, his stakes winning broodmare drops a foal from Big Spruce."

"Big Spruce? He's a leading sire with a really expensive stud fee."

"You got it. So the foal's bred to be a monster runner. As luck would have it, the broodmare dries up. I say…I say luck because now he's got to find a nurse mare. At least, that's what I'm getting from the people on the witness stand before me. He's got a well-bred foal with no momma's milk."

"Right. He's got to nurse the foal to keep it alive. That's not illegal. It happens all the time in the breeding business."

"I say…try shutting up so's I can finish the story."

Monk noticed the sly smile of Victor's sneak across that wretched little face and a tinge of metallic-tasting doubt balled up in the back of his throat, tumbling into his empty stomach and giving him the sensation of driving fast over a small hill. Sometimes, he believed that Victor was putting him on, that the little drunk was not a drunk at all and his semi-literate conversations were smoke screens made of words. But what could an idiot hide? The idea made no more sense than someone executing Red Harvey. He dismissed it with a wave of his hand.

“Go on. I’ve worked all night. I want some sleep before noon.”

“Okay then,” said Victor. “I say…he finds him a nurse mare. She’s a cheap old claimer owned by some Lexington hardboot who’s trying to catch lightning in a bottle and, here’s the tricky part, this ole boy has bred her to some half-assed stud standing on a dirt farm in Henderson, Kentucky. She drops a stillborn foal within days of the Whitney Landis foal, or so the story goes. Whitney gives the hardboot a handful of money, takes the registration papers, which don’t have to be filled out for several more months, and carts the mare back to his place.”

“That’s his nurse mare.”

“Could be. Funny thing or so the story goes. Now, it gets good. Landis claims his expensive broodmare turns her tap back on and weans and raises her own colt. But, the cheap mare he bought suddenly has a colt of her own. So, when it comes time for filling out registration papers on them both and tattooing them so’s they can race in a couple of years, Landis makes the case that the cheap mare’s young healthy colt ain’t worth much because of its bad breeding, and that’s what the registration papers prove, and the tattoo number confirms. Remember, the law says they just have to be identified by tattoo sometime before their first race. Flash forward to the opening week of this race meet. Remember when Red won all that money on a longshot maiden?”

How could Monk forget? “Yeah. It got him married to that hooker named Jane.”

“I say…that was a cheap maiden race, optional claiming for horses worth about five thousand bucks. There wasn’t nothing but plow horses in there, at least on paper. But, some maiden won that damn race easy, went wire to wire and the jockey never uncocked his whip.”

“Sure, I remember. Elvie Coomer dumped a load of money on him right before the bell rang. Had to have a wheel barrow to cart home the winnings.”

"I say…that's just what that crooked bookie fucker bet here. No telling how much he laid off around the country. The maiden belonged to Whitney Landis. It was that bag of bones that come from the nurse mare. Or, was it?"

Victor cackled like a witch and pounded the table with a filthy hand. The daring and scope of the scam and the patience it took to accomplish became clear to Monk, and he spoke slowly.

"The Big Spruce foal is now rumored to be the one the with the cheap tattoo. It looks like the breeding is pure shit. Whitney raises it and puts it in a race where it's sure to outclass everything else. It wins easy. It's like racing a new Corvette against bicycles. He and Elvie take home who knows how much betting money and even if something goes hinky and the stewards smell a rat after the race is over and disqualify the horse, all that can be refunded is the tiny little race purse. What's that, about three thousand bucks? But that sounds like a pretty fucking complicated con to me. Breeding a ringer is a long term process and a lot of shit can go wrong. Besides, the Big Spruce colt is still alive. I read it sold in the Fasig-Tipton sale last year for 125,000 bucks. So where did the other colt come from?"

"You got it. No one knows and no one figured on one of the racing stewards being suspicious enough to get a fraud investigation going. 'Course it could all be bullshit and somebody's trying to muddy up the waters on ole Whitney's governor run with a racing scandal." Victor finished speaking and tried to sneak another Lucky Strike from the open pack on the table.

"So that's what the grand jury's all about."

"Since Red was bragging about all the money he won on that race and since he works for Jack Becker, the guy who trained the winner, he was going to get called for testimony. The prosecutor thought he might know something about the scam. I think them legal types call that a fishing expedition. They subpoenaed me and his other 'known associates' to see if he'd spilled any beans to us. Hell, nobody knew anything at all. I say…I think Red just got lucky. Maybe he heard them talking about how it was a sure thing and took a gamble on it."

"No, I agree. But, what if he heard more than he should have? Is that motive enough for murder?" Victor shrugged his shoulders and Monk went on. "We're talking about hundreds of thousands of dollars and a political future. What about the miracle horse? Where'd it come from?

"Nobody around here knows and they can't prove nothing at this point. The registration and the tattoo match."

"What's this Landis fellow look like?"

As soon as Victor began describing the distinguished looking gentleman from Lexington, Monk recognized him as the man huddled with Elvie Coomer in the court building on Broadway. He also remembered the man with the dead eyes that perched over Landis like a hawk guarding its young. That man was a cold stone killer and the security guard knew it. He was a garbage man, someone hired to taking out the trash efficiently and without attracting attention. On the way out Monk bought a sausage biscuit and sure enough, the mangy little dog was waiting patiently by the door. He fed the poor mutt and thought about how close he was coming to the same lifestyle.

Walking to the end of the long barn area, he climbed in his old truck. Driving slowly down the backside of the racetrack past rows of barns, Monk watched the grooms raking shed rows, cleaning tack, feeding horses, or sitting outside and smoking. There was no longer the pre-dawn chaos. Everyone and everything had settled into his or her singularity of purpose and identity. He had those things once. Playing baseball in high school gave him those things. When he swung a good old Louisville slugger bat and made solid contact with some pitcher's best fastball, the electricity that ran through the wood ran through his body as well. He saw the world for what it was, a Corvette Sting Ray with a turbo-charged engine, and on most days, felt like he was driving it. But that was a fifteen years ago. A man can go through a lot of changes in that amount of time. Hell, a man can go through a lot of changes in ten seconds. His understanding of the simple brightness of life had grown dimmer. His emotions had grown numb and his mind, cluttered with half-thoughts, partial memories, the refuse of survival. What had once been easily definable on a sunlit ball diamond now existed only as shadow. He wasn't who he had hoped to be. What would, could, he do with the information he'd just received from Victor. How could he honor Red's death, a man who claimed him as a friend, a man he knew very little about and liked even less? Yet, the feeling that he owed Red something more than memory was stuck to him like one of those big Saigon River leeches. It wouldn't let go.

He leaned across the seat, keeping his left hand on the steering wheel, and opened the glove box. There was a pack of Lucky Strikes in there, and he wanted one. He had given Victor the open one he carried. At the precise moment the glove box lid came unlatched, the truck hit a hole in the cinder-covered road. Cigarettes fell out along with an old leather ball glove. "Shit, the ballgame. I forgot." He had promised the track chaplain that he would play in the annual charity softball game. Every year the jockeys played the backside workers to raise money for the Horseman's Benevolent and Protective Association and because of his past ability at the game, he had been recruited to help the grooms and hotwalkers try and beat the jocks. That game was due to be played this very evening.

Monk guided the truck over to the grass and stopped. Picking the glove up off the floor, he slid it onto his left hand and pounded his right hand into the well-worn palm. Something came to him with the scent of old leather and Neatsfoot oil, a dim memory of a time when he had been happy. He stared at the frayed stitching on the glove and heard a gentle bark. Outside his truck, the little dog waited. Monk opened the door and his new friend hopped in.

Headline: Time is a River That Only Flows One Way

Two more weeks, the softball game, several evenings of love-making and a reconciliation in his mind about Betsy, several nightmares about Red Harvey mixed up in a jumble of surreal images from the war, four serious hangovers, and three phone calls to Detective Phelps had passed. Phelps had not returned the first two, but with considerable annoyance, agreed to meet Monk off track and unnoticed on the third. The reason for the meeting was simple. Monk had seen Landis and the bookie, Elvie Coomer, in heated discussions with Jack Becker on two occasions and on both, Landis' associate loomed in the shadows. Monk could not get out of his mind the growing dread that somehow these men were responsible for Red's death. He could not erase the thought that someone needed to speak for the little dead man and that he, Monk Johnson, was the only person capable of doing it. The rumors leaking from the grand jury investigation indicated that evidence was insufficient for a fraud indictment, which probably also meant that any connection to the murder was also lost. These assholes might actually get away with everything. Unless something tangible could be found to create a link, Landis might be the next governor of Kentucky.

On the other hand, the racing stewards weren't bound by the same legal restrictions that prosecutors were. They had banned the horse from further racing until they were satisfied it had been correctly identified one way or the other. In a show of good faith, the purse money was refunded and, as mediocre bureaucrats often did, they took the easiest way out. Becker continued racing the other horses in his stable without penalty. Landis agreed to cooperate with the inquiry, saying he was not present when the horse was tattooed and that the day to day operation of the breeding farm fell to his farm manager who may have possibly made an unintentional error because the colts were so similar in appearance. It was a load of crap, but it was politics as usual. At best, Becker would be given a suspension and Landis a fine. Elvie Coomer wouldn't even be involved. Without proving intent to defraud and without proving that Red somehow knew of the plot, which seemed like a long shot and a lot of effort no one was willing to make, the principal players would end up with a slap on the wrist and a bag full of gambling money. Red Harvey would be forgotten just like the mangy dog that was now Monk's constant companion on his nightly rounds.

This reality was unacceptable to the security guard. Maybe it's what drove him to badger Phelps, that and the fact that Monk had learned a long time ago most coincidences were really undiscovered connections. Everything in life connects with everything else. That's how people come to be who they are. A chain of events particular to each individual, both trivial and traumatic, begins at birth and the choices made with every new event get decided based on the results from all preceding events. In this manner, a person's life moves forward in a certain direction. What seems random is really a product of what the unconscious mind remembers and the conscious mind creates a pattern from those images. That was his understanding of the concept of human nature as per delivered by some article in Reader's Digest.

He had never figured out whether some god made those connections possible by creating the events or whether, as his old man used to say, water just naturally seeks its own level, meaning people seek out the circumstances to put themselves in as well. All he knew for sure was that the death of Red Harvey occurring at the precise time a major money player gets caught in an alleged racing fix, particularly involving a horse Red won big money on, must somehow connect. He could feel it in the turgid humidity, hear it in the ugly buzzing of flies around a dead catfish's swollen head, smell it fermenting vegetation along the water's edge as he parked his truck beneath a bridge off River Road and waited for Detective Phelps in their agreed upon meeting spot.

When Joe Phelps arrived a few minutes late, it seemed to Monk that the tall, white-haired man had lost weight and his face, even more wrinkled than the weeks before. The detective was in his shirt sleeves, the suit jacket impossible to wear in the Louisville summer heat. Sweat beaded along his hairline and wet patches covered his white shirt. The tie was loosened and the collar undone. The arrogance was gone also. Phelps looked like a deflated blow up doll of a cop, exhausted physically and emotionally. If crime didn't pay, evidently solving crimes didn't either.

"Make this snappy, Johnson. I haven't been getting any sleep and I'm not in the mood for playing Perry Mason with some would be detective."

"You do look like shit, Phelps."

"In case you haven't heard, the firemen are out on strike. We're pulling double shifts, answering calls, directing traffic at fires, running in looters, and waiting for the National Guard to take over the fire stations, if necessary. I'm not in a real good mood."

"Me either. I think I know who killed Red Harvey and why."

"I told you that case is low priority. Two drunks get in a fight and beat each other silly. One dies, one goes home to sleep it off. Eventually, he'll get drunk again and brag to his friends and we'll run him in and he'll confess. Case closed."

"That doesn't explain the bullet in Red's brain pan."

"One of the drunks had a pistol. Everybody in Kentucky owns a gun."

Monk understood the detective's indifference. It was a numbness that crept over the brain after so much time spent trying to make the world a better place and realizing the world remained the same place it always was. He empathized with Phelps. Only people who had a conscience ever went numb. You believed your actions could make a difference in the wave of violence and injustice that washed constantly over the human race. Monk had felt it himself when he first went to Vietnam. He patrolled the streets, back alleys, brothels, and opium dens of Saigon with determination for a long while during the war. As an MP he felt a responsibility to the soldiers and sailors and marines who came there on R & R from assignments, or worked in the headquarters where a slight misstep could end their lives, where ten seconds of time could age them in terms of years. They drank, smoked, and fucked their way to forgetfulness and he worked diligently against their own inclinations to keep them alive. But after months and months of seeing the same expressions on different faces, the same internal terror of themselves in their eyes when they beat up a hooker, the same impossible regret after an all-night drunk or a bar brawl, and the same realization that they wouldn't be able to keep themselves from repeating their actions when given the next opportunity, he just quit caring. The fear that drove them didn't come from the city or any other outside source. It was born in them. They weren't horrified by what could happen to them but rather by what they had become.

When you understand your actions solve nothing, cure nothing, and ultimately save no one from himself, your conscience dies, and the instinct of survival takes over. It was very similar to swimming in the ocean and getting caught in a riptide. The more you swam against it, the more exhausted you became. At that point, you had two choices. You could quit swimming and drown, or you could swim with the current until you got far enough from shore that it finally let you go. Phelps had begun to swim with the current and when he reached retirement age, if he lived that long, it would finally either let him go or the detective would eat his gun. Monk felt the same things since the war, but the self-medication with whiskey made life bearable, barely. His problem now was Red Harvey. In the man's death, he had thrown Monk a life preserver in this sea of misery, a reawakening of concern, and something vague in the darkest recesses of his primal brain was urging Monk to reach for it.

"I know where you're coming from," said Monk. "I've been there myself."

Phelps rolled his eyes and swatted at a fly buzzing his nose. A line of coal barges drifted by them in the river channel, pushed slowly by a small tug boat. Overhead, the bridge rattled and hummed as traffic crossed from Indiana to Kentucky and back again.

"Oh you think you know, huh? I don't see quite how that would be since you guard piles of horse shit every night."

"You momma ever tell you not to judge a book by its cover. I spent two years working military police and a year with CID in a war zone. If I hadn't been blown to hell with a B-40 rocket during Tet in '68 and come home with a crippled leg, I might be your boss."

Joe Phelps laughed and then laughed again. Monk squirmed from one foot to the other in the hot sun. He put his hand in the pocket of his khaki trousers and grabbed his lucky Zippo lighter. Whenever he was insecure or doubted his own abilities in any circumstance, he had to hold on to the lighter, to feel its realness and with that tangible, visceral connection he was always reminded of the luck it carried in its shell. No one made it in this life without "the luck" and a talisman was needed to hold it captive on your person once you received it.

"Well, I didn't know that. You just moved a few levels upward with me. What's your theory? The least I can do for a vet is listen. I just don't understand why the big concern. There was no evidence of a second person involved, no conspiracy and no apparent premeditation. Probably a bar fight with another transient over a drink. That narrows the field down to a couple a hundred suspects, especially during racing season. Shit happens. Most guys in your job wouldn't put much effort into trying to discover who sent that fellow to the afterlife. You feeling guilty or something?"

Phelps pulled a stainless-steel flask from his back pocket, opened it and offered it to Monk, who drank and instantly felt the calming effect of good bourbon on the body when bad bourbon is wearing off. A slight tingle of joy reached even the constant dull ache in his leg. He handed it back to the cop, who also drank after wiping it off.

Phelps returned to the police cruiser and retrieved a small plastic bag. The bag contained Red Harvey's personal items that were in his pockets—a wallet, some spare change, a broken Case pocketknife, and a blue bandana. In the wallet were two single dollar bills and the creased photo the detective had shown Monk the night they met along with Red's racetrack ID. When Monk glanced at the photo on Red's ID, his mind saw the boy.

The boy stood holding something black in his hand. It was the size and shape of a grenade, and it was Tet in 1968. One round from Monk's .45 lifted the boy off his feet and lifted him in the air slightly like a feather caught an updraft. When the MP got to him, the eyes were open but glazed with the thin veneer of death, and the boy's fingers locked around a sliver of bloody black cloth that held a book of some kind, a photo album. It was at that very moment that Monk began to understand absolutism as a blindness of many colors rather than the absence of them, and every human held all the colors. It wasn't the only person Monk killed during the war, but the memory became the most difficult of them all. Black became white and white faded to gray. The shame drove him to the white room where the shrinks held court when he came home. He had never fully atoned for his sins even though he confessed them. The death of Red Harvey had returned him in his mind to the white room. Attempting to solve this murder was just therapy, another way for a lapsed Catholic to say the rosary.

"Who isn't guilty of something," said Monk. "The thing is, if I don't speak for poor old Red, nobody will. Sure, he was a pain in the ass and he always cheated in a card game, but he would give you the shirt off his back and when he was preaching that Bible nonsense with his buddy, Salvation Sally, it did some good, believe it or not. There's a lot of sad people at the track since he's gone."

"Fair enough. I'll pull Elvie Coomer in and ask him a few questions. Vice has been after his ass for years anyway. Maybe it'll stir something up."

"You know, it wouldn't hurt to pull in that big ugly toad that Whitney Landis has tied to his hip."

"That's his bodyguard. Landis has a lot of pull. I don't like you enough to get my ass chewed out by some bureaucrat who's kissing Landis on the head of his dick hoping that jerk will be governor one day."

"I'm telling you that guy's got dead eyes and a nasty little sneer. He looks like a pit bull somebody put on a chain and beat with a stick just to make sure he'd bite when told to."

"I'll catch him and Whitney at the court building downtown in the morning when Whitney's doing his shyster bullshit and hint around a little bit. Best I can do."

"It'll have to be good enough, then."

"Tell you what. I bet you play poker. Me and a few buddies have a game on Thursday nights in the back room at Willinger's Tavern. You know where that is?"

"Stumbled on it when I was looking for the morgue the other day."

"Why don't you come by and play for a while this week. I'll let you know what I found out then. It's a friendly game, fifty cent ante, dollar limit on raises."

"Deal."

With a flourish of his hand Joe Phelps waved goodbye, slid into the driver's seat of his Crown Victoria and cranked it up. The car spun out from under the bridge moving rapidly along River Road. Monk watched it disappear. He began to like the cop. Their first meeting had been less than friendly. Part of that was Monk's fault. With a constant chip on his shoulder the size of a boulder, it was easy to sound angry even saying hello. But now, Joe Phelps seemed more human being and less authority figure, a man with the same flaws and desires as other men.

Monk stood on the levee. It was so hot the heat became visible rising from the water in shimmering blankets of air. The ground beneath his feet, alive with earthworms and chicken snakes and honeycombed with anthills, had protected Louisville against the feral Ohio ever since the flood of '37 when the bloated river churned through the streets in that year shredding the buildings in front of the floodwall like a giant bulldozer come to crush whole city blocks of concrete and wooden dreams before they were even fully owned.

That was a long time ago, he thought limping the uneven ground toward his old truck. He smelled the world around the water, decaying foliage and dead fish turning over to create new life. Silt and driftwood from unknown origins rushed by atop the current. Brown waves roiled and whitecaps swirled against their alien presence. The swollen liquid hypnotized him for a minute with its constant motion downstream into the Mississippi, into the ocean, and out beyond a vanishing point where the sun and water converged, where nothing and everything met.

Headline: Life Is a Game of Poker

On Thursday he took a vacation day from work. Over the past year, he had earned seven days off with pay, but never knew where to go. The supervisor at the security office let him take his time in small increments. In that way Monk avoided any big decision or the making of specific plans. He found himself lacking the ability to do either since the war, and a poker game with guys who didn't smell like horse shit was as close to a holiday as he seemed able to handle. Freddie would have no trouble dealing with the midweek routine at Churchill Downs by himself. The race meet was more than half over. They were past the Derby and most of the other big events. Secretariat won it and the Triple Crown. The horse became a national hero and America needed a hero badly. The next huge crowd wouldn't arrive till July 4th for closing day. Night shift didn't amount to much except for checking ID's at the gate, putting the occasional drunk to bed, and making sure no one was smoking in the barns. Monk had long been past any particular sense of duty on his job, if he'd ever felt any at all. Only one matter besides sweet Betsy held his interest for more than thirty seconds at a time, Red Harvey's murder, and Phelps would have something for him on that issue soon. Now, if he could only relieve these cops of some money along with information, the night's activities might be well worth his time.

Amateurs and religious nuts viewed poker as gambling, a game where pure luck decided each player's fate. But Monk had played for many years and in rat holes all over the world. He knew better. It wasn't even about the money, really. He'd seen rich men lose their minds over a small change pot and bums never even break a sweat with thousands of dollars in the pot. Winners developed strategies and used them, like a scientist might use a theorem. The best players eventually transcended intellect, learning to trust their instincts. You made bets and drew cards the same way a great artist might choose a certain color or alter a brushstroke because it felt right. You brought an uncluttered mind to the game and felt no concern about the other players to avoid distraction. Above all, you played for love, the love of the game—the way the cards rattled when shuffled and slicked off the deck when you dealt, the way your palms perspired while you waited for the next face up or decided what to discard, the scent of cheap cigar smoke, the mental concentration that led to secret knowledge deep inside the banter, waiting for the mysterious revelation of a tell, and most of all, the rush of blood through your veins that felt like electric current when the hands were turned over after the last call. The risks heightened alertness. Any money you won was a bonus, like finding out your girlfriend had a nymphomaniac sister.

Willinger's Tavern had a back door that led into a small storage room stacked with cases of beer and space in the center for a round, felt-topped table and six chairs. Five of the chairs were occupied when Monk entered. Only two faces were familiar. One belonged to Joe Phelps, who made cursory and quick introductions. Names were far less important in a poker game than facial tics and conversation. Two of the other players, Hank and Billy Ray, worked as cops at Joe's precinct. Jerome, the ghoul from the city morgue, was getting ready to deal to a white-haired guy called Bosco who claimed to own the tavern.

"Sit down, boy. I ain't picked a racetracker's pocket for at least a week," said Bosco, massaging his huge belly with sausage-like fingers. "I shouldn't ate those pickled eggs after dinner. They might be some gas coming in a few minutes."

"You shouldn't eat at all for at least a month," Hank said as he picked up a handful of quarters and restacked them in a new spot.

Jerome shuffled the cards nervously and placed them in front of Billy Ray who cut the deck. Billy Ray pushed the cards back to Jerome, and Monk noticed that his last two fingers were missing on his left hand. He held the hand up and toward Monk.

"I made the sad mistake of a rookie when I joined the force ten years ago. I tried to break up a domestic squabble. The husband had his wife face down on a bar room floor. He was grabbing her by the hair and raising her head and then slamming it back into the floor. Hell, her nose was broke and blood was flying everywhere. I couldn't pry him off, so I sapped him. When he fell sideways, I started to cuff him, and I'll be damned if she didn't crawl over and bite my fingers off. She didn't want me picking on her man."

Billy Ray shook his head and laughed. Monk liked him and recognized at once that he would be hard to read. Experience had taught Billy Ray the hard way to be cautious and not let his emotions direct his actions. As Jerome dealt, Monk extracted a wad of one dollar bills from his shirt pocket and changed ten for a roll of quarters that the banker, Bosco, kept in a shoe box on the floor.

"Dealer calls the game. No wild cards and nothing exotic. Ante's fifty cents and the house keeps a dollar from every pot. But, the beer is on the house and the money covers my overhead," Bosco said.

As if by magic, a pock-faced bartender with dirty blonde hair and skin the same shade of yellow brought in six cold cans of Pabst and placed them on the floor next to the boss man. Bosco tore them one-at-a-time from the plastic rings and passed them around. The cans were ice cold and sweating. Monk felt flushed and happy.

"Five card stud," said Jerome who had already dealt one down and one up to each of the six players around the table. The game was on. The first pot went to Phelps. He drew a king on the last card and that made a pair when added to his one in the hole. Billy Ray had a pair of sevens showing and Monk had an ace in the hole but neither player drew another one. That's the way poker went. You always had hope as long as one more card was coming. Sometimes it paid off and sometimes it didn't, but it kept you betting either way.

The talk was casual, mostly bullshit stories about someone's wife or mistress, about beating black drunks up and down west Broadway on Saturday nights. Jerome regaled the room with tales from the crypt, each story a little more bizarre than the last. At first they were all laughable, dead guys sitting up, surgical instruments left in abdomens, farts and honks. But when Jerome began explaining conversations that he had and winks from female faces Monk thought that spending so much time around corpses had probably driven the skinny coroner bat-shit crazy. Fortunately, it also made him a terrible poker player. He never guarded any facial expressions around dead bodies, so he had lost that ability around the living. Monk could almost recite what cards he held by the twitches and grimaces and smiles. Jerome never won a pot in the first three hours.

Around midnight and after five six packs of beer, the excitement of the game began to wane and tongues flapped freer. Monk was up about fifty bucks. Billy Ray had drawn to an inside straight twice and old fat Bosco had raked in a huge pot with a full house, kings over sevens. Jerome and Hank were the big losers with Phelps breaking about even. Also, the detective nipped from his flask frequently as well as drinking his share of beer. Monk knew Phelps was getting hammered because the old boy had remarked about four times, or each trip to the toilet, how good looking the waitress in the bar room had become as if the blue smoke from their cigarettes and cigars had magically transformed her from troll to princess a little each time he walked through. Joe wasn't alone, though. Billy Ray and Hank's words were beginning to slur. Both men were revealing serious tells now as well. Alcohol made them careless. That's why they bet so many hands without regard to probabilities and lost. When Billy Ray played a strong hand, he never looked at anyone directly. When he played a weak one or bluffed, he scratched his missing fingers as if they itched. Hank had the habit of talking about his mother-in-law whenever he held bad cards. That particular tell was so subtle it might have gone unnoticeable except for the fact that his cards had been so bad all night, she seemed to be his only subject of conversation.

On the other hand, Monk spent so much time every day with his friends Jimmy Beam and Buddy Weiser that a few beers merely topped off his radiator with antifreeze and kept his brain from overheating. He steered the conversation away from wives and dogs and speed boats and the Cardinals toward serious police work. By encouraging the drunken officers to brag, he hoped to draw Phelps out and see whether Whitney Landis' body guard might be a live lead or a dead end, or even if Phelps had any interest in pursuing the matter.

"Is it dangerous being a cop here?" Monk asked, although he already knew the answer. It was dangerous being a cop anywhere. Some places stood out, though. He remembered chasing a Viet Cong teenager through the alleys of Saigon two weeks before the Tet offensive in '68. The kid had just tossed a grenade into a little Pho shop on Hai Ba Trung Street killing the cook and four customers and then sped away on his scooter. They almost lost him in the crowded Ben Thans market district because the jeep contained neither the maneuverability nor the quick pick up of the two-wheeler they were after. His partner, a Spec 4 named Randall Newman, and he saw the kid in the distance. The bomber jumped off and ran into a bar. There had been trouble in this particular bar before and the right thing to do would have been to wait for the Saigon police in their starched and creased little white suits and let them handle it. But the "white mice" were famously inept at everything except taking bribes, and Newman was a cowboy from Texas, who had no patience and very few brain cells.

Slamming on the brakes, the Texan slid the safety off his .45 and headed in the front door. Monk had no choice but to go along. He didn't remember the name of the particular place only that it was in District 1 where a lot of the old whores leftover from the French-Indochina war had set up shop. Monk and the other MP were working in street clothes, khaki trousers and flowered Hawaiian shirts. Had they been in uniform, their entrance would have been greeted with hostile resistance. No military personnel were allowed in bars while in uniform. That order changed after Tet. But at the time, they looked like any of the dozen or so other lowlifes slouched at tables or leaning against the young and beautiful local girls at the bar. In their civvies, they could have been black marketeers, Air America pilots, French expatriates, opium dealers, or construction workers. A loud and scratchy Elvis Presley song about hound dogs blared from the jukebox. The stench of stale beer and urine hung in the heavy cloud of cigarette smoke and mingled with the ammoniac aroma of desperate sweat. A slight, hot breeze churned from three ceiling fans wobbling above them. Even in the dim light and among the sad shadows, Monk could see the boy was absent.

"Where'd the little fucker go," growled Newman, his hand under his shirt at the waist and wrapped around the pistol butt.

"Probably out the back door. Let it go. We'll radio in and get the white mice over here."

"Not a chance. I want that gook son-of-a-bitch myself."

Newman was like one of those big leeches in the Saigon River. Once he latched on to something, he wouldn't let go till blood flowed. It may be where Monk picked up his obsessiveness. In the corner, a disheveled American, sallow and thin with dirty blond hair sipped a Saigon tea. He was leaning back against the wall in his chair, and Monk noticed him smiling. The man, probably a CIA operative, cocked his head toward a closed door behind the bar. As the two MP's approached the locked door, a Vietnamese bartender rushed, waving them off as if he was a traffic cop and they had run a stoplight. Newman, who stood six feet three inches, dwarfed both Monk and the other man. He handed Monk his pistol, grabbed the bartender under both arms lifting him out of the way, tossing him aside like a sandbag. He kicked the door, and it splintered at the lock. Monk checked behind them. Every customer accepted random violence as part of daily life. Consequently, no one paid any attention to the little drama acting out a few feet away from them. Involving yourself in a confrontation that was none of your business could get you killed quickly in Saigon and they all knew it.

The broken door opened into a storage room not unlike the one where Monk now sat playing poker ten years later. The difference lay in the fact that this room had no back door and yet, the bomber boy seemed to have disappeared from it. They tossed aside cases of LaRue beer and Tiger beer. They restacked broken patio furniture and dusty faux French art leftover from the 1950's. One bare light bulb swung on a wire and, covered with dead bugs and soot, shown dimly overhead. The floor was nothing more than dirt packed hard by rubber-soled foot traffic going back a hundred years. Monk took his flashlight and began tapping the walls. Still, nothing. In one corner and looking a little out of place sort of like a one legged man at an ass kicking contest, a small chiffonier from some French planter's bedroom caught Monk's eye. It wasn't large enough to hold a man, but maybe a Vietnamese boy. The hair on the back of his neck stood up and pressure built at the base of his skull. That feeling had pulled him back from the edge of an abyss more than once. He trusted it.

But when Monk opened the door, Newman laughed.

"We got us a regular gook Houdini," the big Texan said. "That's the last place anyone could hide."

But the shelves held neatly stacked bags of opium, which is exactly what the bartender had been trying to protect. The little man had no idea that the MP's weren't interested in dope.

"Now what?" asked Monk.

"I guess we'll do what you wanted to in the first place."

"Yeah, we'll go get back in the jeep and let their own cops sort things out."

"Aren't you the least bit curious how the kid got out? Let's go beat the shit out of the bartender until he tells us."

"And then I'll have to fill out paper work for two hours. No way."

Monk felt a tinge of disappointment as he placed his own .45 back on safety and holstered it under his shirt. His neck hairs had never lied. Whenever he felt the blood rush up his spine, he could always count on some excitement, and the high that came with it was like injecting a powerful opiate. He didn't understand the complex psychological conflicts that created the euphoria during and the guilt after each event, but the thrill had become addictive.

They walked back into the main bar area and threaded their way through an increasingly chaotic crowd. The blond-haired tipster had disappeared. The new faces were Vietnamese and Chinese. In one corner a table full of taxi dancers and ARVN soldiers waved at him. Monk waved back as if the dance floor were not an ocean, as if he had not already drowned them all in his numbed mind.

A hiss of escaping air—a whispered "why"— almost like the beating of dragonfly wings buzzed in his ear. He whirled to meet it and saw Newman three steps behind him clutching over his shoulder at his back. The big man fell face down as the crowd fell silent. Petals of blood flowered open across Newman's white shirt.

The boy bomber must have been at one of the tables, or under it. No one moved, not even the ARVN regulars with weapons, except for a blur in the corner of Monk's right eye. The Viet Cong boy was on him with a K-Bar knife in hand. The same one that must have just punctured Newman's lung and probably nicked his aortic artery. As the boy prepared to bring the blade across his throat, Monk threw his right arm up in an L and caught the boy's arm in a block. With his left arm, he grabbed the hilt and the boy's hand. Dropping his right, he rammed the elbow into his enemy's solar plexus. The boy grunted loudly and the force of Monk's blow lifted his tiny but wiry frame off the ground slightly.

Bringing the arm straight up and back, his fist smashed into soft nose cartilage with a splat. Simultaneously, Monk tightened his grip on the knife hilt and let the boy stumble backward a step. Monk bent low, lifted the boy over his back with a classic judo throw and onto a near-by table. The table's legs gave way. As his opponent, tangled in chair legs and tablecloths fell to the floor and struggled to raise himself, Monk reached under his shirt in one fluid motion, clicked the safety off the .45, pointed, and fired. The loud explosion echoed through the room. People ran for the door, even the ARVN soldiers. The boy caught the round mid-chest and dropped straight down, dead before he hit the floor.

Monk looked at both bodies. He tried to dismantle the chaos drowning his mind into understandable pieces It made no sense. The boy was home free. Newman and Monk were leaving the place. Wherever he hid, it had fooled them. There was simply no reason for the attack. And that, Monk decided, was what made all police work everywhere dangerous. You could never account for the actions of other people. They would fool you in the most unreasonable and illogical ways. Just like a woman would bite the fingers off a cop who saved her life, just like a kid that had escaped capture would sacrifice his freedom and his life. Without warning people would make life-threatening decisions based on no discernible motive. Until cops could read minds or see the future, they risked their lives every time they said hello to a stranger.

"This city isn't near as bad as Detroit or Chicago for cops. But, we do have out share of danger for the citizenry," said Hank. "Ask ole Joe. He's been trailing a killer for the last three years."

Billy Ray snorted. Phelps gave Hank a withering look. Bosco rolled his eyes and began dealing another hand, although his movements had slowed considerably from the alcohol and the sleep deprivation. The smoke was so heavy over the poker table that everyone's eyes watered and were shaded pink. Jerome scratched his head and spoke.

"You never did catch the tattoo killer, did you, Phelps?"

"The tattoo killer?" Monk said, looking at a pair of Jacks Bosco had just dealt him.

"That's a bullshit name some lame ass newspaper reporter thought up after the third attack. We don't even know if it's the same guy," Phelps said.

"Same MO," said Hank. "All three of the women were hookers that no one would really miss that much, and each one got shot while Churchill Downs was open and running a meet."

"With the same caliber gun," Phelps interjected.

"Similar, similar. Besides, the third girl wasn't murdered, and she's the one that gave us the tattoo. It's just good speculation if the same guy killed the first two because we got no witnesses,"

Billy Ray spoke while looking at his cards.

"How about the body delivered to the morgue a few weeks ago right after the race meet opened. That's the fourth woman. You got to admit, the timing is a pattern," Jerome said and opened the betting with a dollar and a quarter to Billy Ray.

"What kind of pattern?" Monk asked Phelps directly and the detective answered as he folded his poker hand without ever betting.

"It may all be a coincidence. But every one of the victims was shot during a current race meet."

"That doesn't connect with Red Harvey. He was male and that breaks the pattern," Hank said.

Jerome nodded his head, as did Joe Phelps and Billy Ray. Then, Jerome responded. "Certainly true, but the victims including the man were all throw-a-way people and they all had .22 caliber bullets in the head."

"Your theory's full of shit. First, the world is full of .22 caliber guns. Second, you don't have any way to prove the bullets matched because the ones you recovered were too damaged. Third, Red Harvey was a drunk racetracker who got beat up, probably by another drunk racetracker, over a stolen bottle of booze or something worth even less. His head shot was a coup de gras delivered for some deranged reason we'll never figure out. These other murders were methodical and fairly precise, all neighborhoods around 18th and Market where the pro's worked."

The players had set their cards down and stared at Phelps as he finished his rant. Monk could see the whole case was a sore spot to the detective, and he understood. Still the death of Red left him with some questions that no one seemed interested in answering. He understood that as well.

"Point taken, Phelps," said Jerome.

"Let's get back to cards, and maybe you need to realize that police work is for men, not ghouls."

Billy Ray rubbed the nubs of his two missing fingers as he spoke and watched Jerome closely, waiting for the mortician to bet. Monk could tell Billy Ray was anxious, which probably meant the cop held good cards in his hand.

"You don't believe that," said Bosco. "You're just mad cause you haven't caught him.

Hank added one thought. "It is strange that Churchill Downs is always open for the summer meet and the perp has always forced them on their knees first, like he's going to get a blow job. But he shoots them instead. The hooker that lived said she was more than willing if it would save her life, but she never got the chance. She said he started crying and boom. It all went dark. Weird, man, really weird. She was in a coma for three weeks."

Jerome threw a buck and into the pot and with an afterthought added another dollar to raise Billy Ray. “Don’t forget he always kills them the same way, with a .22 round in the head. The bullet just gets so mangled up in there you can’t tell anything specific about it.”

That’s also how you leave someone alive, thought Monk. If you’re not real good with a gun, or you hand’s a little shaky, and you don’t put the kill shot in the kill spot, the caliber of the slug is small enough some people don’t die. He called Jerome’s raise as did Billy Ray. Hank and Bosco folded, like Phelps. Bosco dealt more cards to the three players and collected their discards. Even though he had held a pair of jacks and collected three new cards, Monk was completely disinterested in the game now.

“I still don’t get where the tattoo killer thing came from. And if it’s related to the race meet?” Monk asked.

“When we interviewed the girl, she told us there was a tattoo, now get this, a tattoo of a huge eye ball with a single tear falling out of it located below the guy’s navel and above his pubic hair. It’s like the eye was crying on his penis,” said Phelps.

“Man, that’s one sick puppy,” Bosco added. “What happened to the good old days when you just paid some toothless hooker five bucks for a good head job and both of you then went on about your business.”

“Anyway, that detail was held back from the newspapers, but they had a field day with some other leaked info. The chief thought it was me since I was lead on the case, and I almost lost my shield.”

“Yeah, but it wasn’t and you didn’t, so let’s finished the goddamn hand and go home.” Billy Ray yawned after he spoke. “There’s always one case that sticks in your craw. This one’s gonna be yours, Joe.

“By the way,” said Jerome, “I’m done with old Red Harvey and so is the coroner. Officially, it’s a homicide. Cause of death was the bullet to the head. The blunt force trauma from a heavy wooden object, most likely a baseball bat, was superfluous, like the fifth shot of tequila.”

Headline: Who's Your Daddy?

If you happen to be a little OCD as Monk could be, some thoughts get stuck in your brain and you can't unthink them, at least till you're satisfied with a conclusion of some kind. He laid awake for hours after the poker game. His sleeping room at Jody's felt like a prison cell and in the darkness that surrounded him, in the spinning noise of crickets outside his screened window, in the hum of tires from an occasional passing car, in the flash of headlights as they passed, tattoos refused to go away. Phelps could identify his serial killer with a tattoo. A tattoo could be a work of art, a sign of love, a warning, a plea for redemption, many things. But tattoos were also a way to identify people, unique like a fingerprint. More than that, tattoos told a careful observer not just who the person was but something about their personalities as well. He thought of what Red's DI BO CHET tattoo told him about Red as a person that he could have never surmised through conversation. No one ever had the exact same one in the exact same place, and that uniqueness qualified as proof of someone's individuality in one way or another.

A story he read once in a book about World War II spoke of twin brothers, Jews swept up in the tide of hatred in Germany and sent to Dachau. The twins were identical in physical appearance. They both lived. After the liberation, the twins immigrated to America only to be killed by an apartment building fire ten years later in New York City. Authorities had no way of telling which brother was which till some savvy morgue director thought of researching the barely visible remains of different tattoo numbers on each of their arms and comparing those numbers with historical records recovered from the death camp. The difference in those numbers proved that, although the brothers appeared the same, they were different. It may not have seemed all that important to most people, after all they were both dead. However, Monk appreciated not only the irony, but the dignity it gave both men to be acknowledged for who they were in life.

Sleep never came. He lay impatiently with his eyes wide open and watched the first gray light of the new day crawl over his windowsill and across the floor. Maybe Doc Tandini could spare him a minute or two before starting his morning rounds.

Headline: A Nasty but Necessary Narrative Digression

In the instant of his utmost pleasure, Hoss knew he was going to hell. He knew it and he didn't give a damn. Rubbing the top of the woman's head gently, as if she was his favorite dog, he stared at the ceiling in the feed shed. His five-dollar donation to the ministry of the crazy preacher woman who cleaned stalls for Todd Blanchard's stable had gone a long way. She had been hollering up a storm at the track kitchen before it was even light, like she always did before work. Most people paid her a few coins to go away, but some were more generous if she promised to bless them in return.

She usually waited till there was a bigger crowd later in the morning after the horses had been exercised, cooled out, and done up for the day. There was always that time between then and the first race in the afternoon when all the backstretch workers came to the kitchen to eat, play cards, read the Racing Form, or hustle for hot gambling tips. She must have been real short on money to start begging for donations this early. Most men would have paid for a blow job without any thought to religion, but Hoss had developed a conscience early in life before he ran away to the track. He could never approach her and simply ask to receive head like a communion wafer, all the while knowing her holiness and divine calling. So, he whispered a question. "How much would it cost me to see Jesus this morning?"

At the barn, horses whinnied, stomped, and rattled their feed tubs up and down the shed row. That sound meant Victor was out of the tack room and shuffling toward the feed shed for a bucket of oats. It must be 6A.M. – breakfast time. "Hurry baby, suck it good, suck it good." The woman grunted. The door creaked open.

"Fuck me, I say fuck me," said Victor and dropped the empty bucket. Startled, the preacher jerked her head upward, skinning Hoss's dick with her teeth.

"Goddamnit." A little blood seeped from the sides, but nothing else came out.

"Hey, how come you didn't wake me for some," said Victor.

"Some what? Get the fuck out, get the fuck out. I was coming."

"Some of that sweet little Christian breakfast."

"Donate brother. You got to donate."

"Fuck you. I'll donate alright. Hell, you're so fat. So fat I say that you can't even see your own cock. You might have a dog licking it instead of her," said Victor as he unfastened his pants and struggled to find the zipper. As he dropped his pants to his knees, the preacher woman looked up to see Victor's navel and below that a half-hard penis.

"Jesus saves," screamed the preacher woman and squeezed past Hoss' fat belly out the door and into the barn area. Two stallions charged their stall webbings, thrusting massive chests against the nylon. The whole barn shook. Two fillies whirled in their stalls and kicked the back walls with a loud crack. The woman ran across the road past the muck pit and toward the track kitchen.

"I say, I say you ain't got a mouthful. She's going for breakfast to get a real meal."

"I guess you better shut up. Shut up. Now what I got is blue ball." Hoss grabbed the empty bucket, scooped it full of rolled oats, and threw Victor the plastic feed cup. The entire stable of horses was agitated when the boss walked around the corner.

"What the hell's going on? Get these horses fed you jack asses. You're late. I want the bandages pulled while their eating. Victor, let

Hoss feed them. You fill the water buckets and hang them on the outside rail."

"You want electrolytes in the clean water boss?"

"What's the matter with you? Why are you asking me stupid questions? I swear to God, you're both nuts."

Hoss giggled and squealed like a little girl as Victor went into the tack room to find the container of electrolytes. The fat man's dick stung from the skinning, his balls ached, but his mind felt light and painless. After he finished the water buckets, he would go tell his favorite horse, Beau Geste, of his good fortune. Even though horses don't talk—well, except that one at Oaklawn Park last winter that recited the Lord's Prayer when Hoss had been hiding in the stall from his dead grandma who came back to life after he spent three days without drinking because no one would buy him any beer, and that funny horse on TV named Ed—Hoss knew that old Beau would love to hear a good sex story. He had been with the horse for three years now, not as long as he'd been with Victor, but longer than any other relationship in his life

Headline: The Doctor Is In

9 AM, Friday, June 15 1973:

"Hey Doc. Got a minute."

"What's up, Monk?"

Doc Tandini had parked his Cadillac on the gravel path in front of the barn that housed Winston Hughes and his large stable of twenty-plus horses. Monk liked the jovial old trainer, Hughes. He chewed on an unlight cigar and was nearly always laughing at something. Monk wished that attitude was contagious. The trunk lid opened, and Doc stood by the rear bumper checking a notebook before extracting any medicine or equipment from it. His forehead dripped with beads of sweat from under the brim of a porkpie hat and his tan coveralls were soaked through under his arms. The sun reflected brightly off the snowflake white chat path and Doc squinted to read whatever was printed in his notebook. He stopped and stared at Monk's blanched face.

"Rough night?"

"No sleep. I hate being alone with my thoughts sometimes."

"Everybody does. That's why God invented good-looking women. So we don't have to do much thinking if we keep them around. Of course, my wife says I'm incapable of rational thought when I'm sober anyway." Doc chuckled as if his comment was almost funny.

"Twins…I was thinking about twins."

"Now that's a great image, good-looking twins."

"Not women, do mares ever have twins?

"Rarely."

"Are they allowed to race?"

"As long as they both get registered listing the Dam, the sire, the date, their color and any specific markings. That usually happens before they're a year old. Then, the Thoroughbred Racing Protective Bureau sends a technician to tattoo them on the underside of the upper lip that links them to their papers. One letter and five random numbers. The letter stands for the year beginning with A and running through the alphabet to Z. Then it begins again. It's 1973 and we're on C again. It's pretty much foolproof."

Monk leaned against the Caddy's rear fender, took off his Chicago Cubs baseball cap, and ran his fingers through his dark brown hair. Islands of fluffy cumulus clouds floated in the blue sky and a low sun heated the car's metal enough that his tee-shirt soaked through with sweat almost immediately. It might have been a perfect day for a picnic or a murder.

"Nothing's foolproof. What if you separated the twins and listed them by different sires."

Doc smiled. Gazing first at Monk and then into the trunk of his car. He extracted a vial of Phenylbutazone and two syringes from a metal tray as he spoke.

"That's an old myth and a probability that would mostly likely never occur. First, it's a crime, and I don't see much of a motivation."

"Why not? Couldn't you create a ringer that way. You know, a well-bred horse running as a cheap claimer would have a good chance of beating the field."

"Maybe, but you'd have to be very patient because you're talking about waiting the two or three years it takes to get the horse to the races without injuries, and then you have to remember the best horse doesn't always win. There's a lot of variables for a small amount of purse money."

"But it could happen."

"Not really. The only case that I know of when twins both made it to the races was 1959. Stop on Red and Go on Green were twins and they each ended up winning seven races before retiring. Here's why. It's an anomaly and dangerous. Eighty per cent of the mares pregnant with twins ends up miscarrying at least one within the first forty days. If they make past that, the vet is forced to abort one because the mare has room for the weight of only one in the womb. That means the other one, if alive to term is going to be sickly, crippled, and underweight. Yes, your theory may be possible but only if you believe in miracles like me hooking up with Farah Fawcett. Why are you so interested? Hurry up. I've got work to do."

"I'm doing research for my PhD in Nonsensical Probability."

As Monk turned to walk away, Doc yelled "asshole." Monk lifted his arm and with a wave of his hand as he walked toward the track kitchen. Riders and horses from various barns made their way slowly to the back gap in the racetrack fence. Some pranced and scooted along feeling better about the morning workout than others that plodded, heads down and bored, with the monotony of another gallop around the same oval on yet another hot, tiresome day. Monk stumbled on the loose gravel and for an instant thought he might have felt the earth spinning ever so slightly on its way through the day.

Headline: Life Doesn't Always Happen the Way You Think It Will

Friday night passed slowly and uneventfully, the monotony broken only by the stench of Frank's gas filling the humid air of the guard shack and the occasional horse trailer bringing in some runners for the next day's race card. Monk had to send one poor bastard all the way back to River Downs in Cincinnati because the horse's Coggins test was expired. He felt bad for the trainer, some poor old gypsy with a cheap claimer trying to take purse money by beating the big stables and their expensive horses. But rules were rules. No way was Monk Johnson going to let an infected horse on the track. It should have been an ethical decision—what's right is right and what's wrong is wrong. But ethics and morality became secondary concerns after Vietnam. If he learned anything in the military, it was survival first—shit rolls downhill. As low man in the pecking order whatever went wrong would be his fault. The people that ran the place seemed long on profit incentive. They would fire him in an instant for a mistake that might cause them a lawsuit. On the other hand, he wasn't without a moral compass. He would never endanger innocent horses with a virulent virus that could end a racing career and maybe even cause them to be euthanized.

The virus was called Swamp Fever, a form of encephalitis particular to horses and donkeys. A veterinarian from Cornell University had isolated it in 1970 and developed a blood test for it. Since then, every racetrack in the country required thoroughbred trainers to provide proof from a licensed vet that the test had been administered and the horse in question proved negative, or security could not allow the horse inside the gates of the racetrack. One infected horse bitten by a single mosquito who then bit another horse could start an epidemic. Stables would be ruined, the small businesses that profited from race meets bankrupted, and hundreds of employees laid off. It was a nightmare scenario that Monk's slightly paranoid conscience would never let happen.

At 5 a.m. darkness receded into the horizon like hot black tar seeps into a crack on an asphalt highway, replaced by the faded gray of another pre-sunrise morning. Monk made his final walking round as grooms and horsemen began to arrive at their barns. Horses whinnied and stomped in stalls, eager for a cup of oats. Exercise riders dragged saddles and bridles from tack rooms where bare light bulbs had just popped on. The air filled with the acidic tang of urine-soaked straw and liniment. He liked this time best of all. Most of the barns had at least two or three people working in them who knew him and waved or yelled "morning" as he passed. Dawn was a time full of promise and expectation even if you'd been awake all night. Walking the corridor of familiar faces was the closest experience he had these days to belonging, and it was enough.

Considering the conversation with Doc Tandini in his mind, he remembered the numbers inked on the back of Red's wedding photo that Joe Phelps had shown him that first morning after Red's death. Z59324. The tattoo had been done in 1970. It identified a specific horse and Red wrote down the number. How did he get the number and what did it mean and how did it fit with Monk's idea about twins? This puzzle might also explain why Red ended up dead.

Approaching the guard shack to clock out a few minutes before six, he saw Frank speaking to a tall man in a black suit leaning against of an unmarked police cruiser. Monk recognized Joe Phelps immediately. He had an arrogant smile of power and a malignant type of condescending stare made all the more irritating because Monk pictured the rest of the Joe's face belonging to a burned out surfer from a distant beach. A pure white mane, and mane is the best word Monk could think of, topped the man's thin body. The hair had the textured sheen of expensive silk and it framed a peanut butter colored face that included a firmly set square jaw. The skin, damaged by long term exposure to sunlight, resembled a paper bag. It was as if someone or something had wadded it up and then tried to smooth it before gluing it over his skull. The total look was incongruous, and he knew from personal experience that Phelps was an okay guy for having spent thirty years as a cop. Monk liked details in their place. It made life simpler.

What brought Louisville's finest to his domain on this morning? Some race tracker had probably been arrested for drunkenness the previous night or the cop was looking for a runaway. Like the carnival, the racetrack was a good place to escape a drunken father, molesting stepfather, trip to rehab, truant officers, or maybe an arrest warrant for dealing drugs. Consequently, it was full of teenagers and lost souls, and those two things were not mutually exclusive. Sometimes the lost souls were teenagers. When hungover, he felt as if the label "lost" would apply very nicely beside his own name.

Frank's uniform was soaked in sweat, and the fat man kept shifting back and forth from one foot to the other as if he'd crapped his pants.

The detective seemed to smile, but it stretched across his face as more of a grimace than an expression of joy.

"Morning Monk," the cop said.

"At least you had the courtesy to not say good morning," said Monk and wished he had a half-pint of Jim Beam close by.

"What are you grumping about. You left the game up fifty bucks Thursday night. Do you recognize this man?"

The detective stuck a wrinkled Polaroid photo in his face. Monk winced.

"Hey, cop guy is back," said Frank.

"That much is obvious. Why don't you go finish the night reports before the morning supervisor gets here looking for something to bitch about?"

Disappointed, Frank waddled off toward the guard shack at the 4th Street entrance. Phelps turned the picture over and Monk saw scribbling on the back that he conjectured to be writing. As he squinted in the early morning sunlight, the faded ink scratches began to focus and separate into letters. Monk made out the few words. *Me and my friend Red Harvey. Churchill Downs. 1973, Spring Meet.*

"Yeah, yeah…that's a groom named Butch Chernov that was best man when Red Harvey got married to a hooker for about three days. I think I told you that when you showed me the wedding picture you found on Red's body. Chernov is another drunk and with a bad temper."

"When's the last time you saw him?"

"Two weeks ago when I put him in an ambulance. He was babbling and not wearing a stitch of clothes. Had a bad case of DT's. He claimed somebody stole his whiskey and his money. He threatened several people with murder before he started hallucinating and when some of them complained, the HBPA had him ruled off the track. The stewards revoked his license."

"And you haven't seen him since, right?"

"Jesus Joe, I said no once already."

"I followed your tip on our future governor's bodyguard and that guy is a real piece of work. He was connected with the Phoenix Program in 'Nam. Problem is, he was doing his job in Frankfort when old Red Harvey got beat to a pulp and then shot. Our next governor was at a dinner kissing big-donor ass. So that let's Whitney Landis and this doofus Robert Franklin Goss off the hook for murder."

"What about the gunshot wound to the head?"

"What about it? It was a murder, but most prosecutors aren't going to waste the resources on more investigation and a big trial for an itinerant like Red Harvey, especially if we got a guy already who fits the bill. Besides that, we're understaffed, and the police department isn't going to prioritize this case over a dozen others.

"What's your interest in Chernov?"

"Patrol ran him in last night. They stopped him on the Watterson Expressway weaving all over the road in an old Chevy. He was drunk as a skunk. Thing is, he had a sawed-off Louisville Slugger with a lead-filled top and the bat was covered in blood. The dumb ass hadn't even wiped it clean. We're testing to see if it matches Red Harvey's. If it does, I got a bartender that's willing to say he saw them arguing over whiskey the night of the murder. The place is on Broadway a few blocks from the alley where the body was dumped. It's called Freddy's Lounge."

"Yeah, I know it. It's an old bar close to Jefferson College downtown. Alkies like it because it's open till three in the morning and re-opens at six o'clock."

"Sounds like you know it pretty well."

"What about a gun, or a reason why Chernov would beat someone and then also shoot him?"

"Maybe he was in a drunken stupor and forgot he already beat the guy. Maybe he threw the gun in the Ohio River. Who knows? It's an easy closure for us, so who really cares?"

"Yeah, but is it justice?"

Phelps repeated the word justice in a whisper and drove off laughing.

Headline: Can a Mind Get Casted?

Joe Phelps had been right on both counts. For most people finding someone who could be labeled the killer would be enough for most cops, and Monk was too familiar with nasty bars and the lowlifes that inhabited them. But Monk needed closure. He developed an obsessive-compulsive need for patterns and organization about certain things during the war. He was never sure why or what those things might be, but when they popped into his mind, he just couldn't let them go till they were right. It might be something simple, like putting the ketchup bottle down at a restaurant. The label had to be facing him or he had to turn it till it did. If he went to a movie or sat anywhere in a crowd, his back had to be against a wall, or if outside, against a tree so he could survey the area. At least once a day he counted backward from a hundred by seven's because he read that some doctors used that as a test for Alzheimer's disease. Or it could be something big, like how and why Red Harvey caught a bullet in the brain pan after he was beaten with a bat. That little nag in the back of his mind would grow larger and larger. It would dominate his thoughts until he knew the answer. He wouldn't be able to drink, sleep, or fuck it away. When he coupled that with his theory that Whitney Landis was an entitled pervert who owned a horse breeding farm capable of breeding twins, the perception that horse race cheating and Red Harvey's murder were connected was branded into his back brain. It was short work for his synapses to build a bridge between the left-side logic and the right-side intuition parts of his brain as well.

As to Joe's dig at his lifestyle. Well and hell, he was working on that. Saturday was his day off and Betsy didn't work the evening shift at J.C.'s. He had made serious plans for a serious dinner with her at a nice place where he could test the waters, so to speak, on their new relationship. Was it even a relationship at this point? Did she foresee a future for them? Did she want a future? Did Monk want one? He had been through two marriages already at the age of thirty-two. Both were short-lived and both were products of something other than love. They happened after he came home from Vietnam and seemed to have occurred to fill a vague need in his mind rather than a desire in his heart.

The first simply reconnected him with a high school sweetheart and was nothing more than the fulfillment of a Midwestern cliché. They were going steady when he left for boot camp. She wrote him while he was gone, and they got engaged two weeks after his discharge. The war left him with an emotional numbness. He didn't feel much for his fiancé. He didn't feel much about anything. After a few months of fucking, they got married because Monk thought that's what normal people did. He struggled to feel normal. After six months of that struggle, he found he hated his job at the Whirlpool factory, his former friends who had avoided the draft disgusted him, and Karen, his wife, could barely get him hard. The electricity was gone, from their bed, from his life. Monk wanted to feel the adrenaline that came in the darkness patrolling those Saigon alleyways, the uncertainty of life and the terrible fear of death. It existed nowhere anymore and so, he substituted it for a bar stool at the White Horse Tavern. He drank till she left.

The second marriage resulted from guilt and lasted less time than the first. He was twenty-three years old at the time and working as an apprentice to a carpet-layer in upstate New York. He drifted from the Midwest to the Catskills after his fiasco with Karen because he had never been there and found the job offer in the classified section of the Middletown newspaper. His boss, Tony, hired him on the spot. Tony was a veteran and liked to hire veterans. Tony had a nineteen-year-old daughter. Marie loved sex and was part of a generation that created a revolution by making the act of sex a casual undertaking, like shaking hands with a new acquaintance. But Monk began to feel guilty working everyday while Tony bragged on her virtuous behavior and how she was saving herself for the right man. After a couple of months of being filled with a Puritanical shame instilled in him by his mother as a teenager, he could no longer look his boss in the eye. The couple had a big Italian wedding. Two weeks later, Marie ran off with the pizza delivery driver and Tony had the church annul the wedding. Monk drifted south.

He had thought of relationships in terms of days ever since. Now, Betsy made him almost believe in love. He punched his timecard and headed for the track kitchen and one last cup of coffee when trainer Smiley Adams wheeled his new Chevy pickup truck off Fourth Street and squealed to a stop at the back gate. The guard waved Smiley through, and the truck's tires whined as they spun across the concrete.

"Hey Charlie," Monk yelled back over his shoulder. "Smiley's gunning that truck is going to spook a horse and get someone hurt."

RHIP—An old military acronym bolted through his mind, one often repeated by low-ranking enlisted personnel who he busted for some offense as they watched MP's ignore the same offense committed by officers. Rank has its privileges. Certainly unfair, but it remained a status quo in most areas of life. Smiley Adams, by virtue of having a forty-horse stable including some expensively-bred allowance and stakes contenders and by virtue of running those horses frequently, which filled racing cards and brought in bettors, had become a formidable presence at most racetracks on the Midwest circuit. Those tracks included Churchill. Smiley did what he damn well pleased most of the time. People who exploited their power irritated Monk.

"He's got a horse casted. His barn foreman ran up to the shack a few minutes ago and asked us to call his apartment and get him over here ASAP," Charlie answered.

Okay, maybe Smiley had a legitimate reason to be in a hurry. Thoroughbreds are valuable animals and for most of the people on the racetrack provided their only means of livelihood. An injured horse could not train or perform. Like any other professional athlete, they had to be kept fit and healthy. A casted horse was in a dangerous predicament.

Thoroughbreds were beautiful, graceful, fast, and stupid. A trainer's job consisted of not only keeping them healthy but conditioning them to the edge of insanity. After arriving at a high level of fitness, they became a bundle of energy that lived in a twelve foot by twelve-foot stall for twenty-three hours a day rather than an open pasture. Unfortunately, their instincts remained geared for open spaces. They sometimes became fractious and playful, rolling in the straw bedding as if it were a field of clover. If they wallowed on their backs, got close to one of the four walls, and then tried to stand completing the roll in the wrong direction, all four legs could wind up pinned against a wall, The action left them trapped like a turtle on its back. The difference was that they panicked violently, kicking, squealing, snorting, and often injuring one of their thin, fragile legs in the unsuccessful struggle for leverage until exhausting themselves. It often required two or three people to pull them away from the wall so they could stand, which was also dangerous to the men in the stalls because the horses rose wildly and thrashed around the enclosed space. A thousand-pound horse can do a lot of damage to itself and others. Exercises in poor judgment must be a flaw in all species, thought Monk. He went to his apartment for sleep hoping Smiley's horse had been rescued, but not for Smiley's sake. Fuck Smiley.

Headline: Horsemen Bring Your Horses to the Paddock for the Next Race

After four hours of restless sleep, Monk called Joe Phelps. The detective was at his desk in the precinct office downtown.

"What do you want. I'm busy with a shit-ton of paperwork," said the detective.

"Then get a real job."

"Fuck you."

They both laughed as if they were still teenagers without the scars that come in adulthood. Monk guessed that in a different time and a different world he and Phelps might have become close friends, but the burdens they both carried prevented the trust required for such a bond.

"Have you made any progress with Chernov?

"That's the report I'm working on now. Blood type on the bat is a match for Red Harvey. Chernov broke down in the box and cried like a baby. He swore that he didn't mean to kill anybody. Evidently, he confronted Red about a pint of whiskey stolen from him and Red told him to get lost. Chernov left and sat in his truck sipping Seagram's Seven till Red Harvey left the bar at closing. Then, he took a bat from under the seat and worked the guy over. Said he just wanted to remind him that it was wrong to steal."

"Well, he didn't have to send him all the way to Jesus for the reminder."

Monk was shaking his head in disbelief while holding the phone to his ear. Men seemed to get more vicious the smaller the stakes. It never made sense to him.

"What about the gunshot to the head?"

"After the fact by a few minutes. That's one of the reasons we didn't notice it at first. Not much blood leakage. Butchy-boy didn't have a gun or any gunshot residue on his unwashed body or clothes, so someone else was in that alley. This is probably going to become another cold case for the files. Like I told you before, no District Attorney is going to waste the city's meager resources in a major investigation for the killer of a bum who might have died from the beating later anyway. And, Chernov swears Red Harvey was sitting up mumbling when he left the alley. The bullet was definitely .22 caliber, but it got so messed up rattling around inside the skull there'd be no way to get a match, and we got no leads."

"I get that. But it's still bugging me because somebody wanted to make sure Red was dead. I'd like to know why, especially if Whitney Landis had the balls to order his bodyguard to make sure Red never testified about race fixing to a grand jury."

"Let it go, Monk. You've got no power or reason to investigate."

"Curiosity."

"Curiosity killed a cat, and it can kill a security guard. That guy who works for Landis is the real deal. Now leave me alone and leave this alone."

The call ended with Monk Johnson both sad and angry. No one would speak for Red Harvey now. Chernov beat him in a typical argument for these guys over booze. It happened occasionally on the racetrack. But somebody executed Red. Intent was important to Monk. What a person wanted to do, positive or negative, said a lot about that person's character. If Landis hoped to be the next governor of Kentucky, it would be nice to know if the politician had a murderous soul before the election if only for his own piece of mind. He had understood since his military police days that corruption was the way of life for many people, especially in politics. But rule by graft and rule by terror were not on the same scale.

After the phone call, Monk checked the time. It was 3PM on Saturday, June 16, 1973. A big day at Churchill Downs, the Governor's Handicap. The Derby was over and there were only two weeks left in the spring meet. Secretariat went on to win the Preakness, and on the previous Saturday Big Red had destroyed the field in the Belmont Stakes by 34 lengths making sure of his place in history as a winner of the Triple Crown. The horse had become a national hero at a time when America begged desperately for one, thought Monk. A hero appeared. A force, call it fate or destiny, seemed to be at work in this instance that could not be denied.

By the end of the first week of July the track would be emptied of most horses. Stables would ship to other tracks for summer meets lasting six to eight weeks, some more, leaving only flies. His duties on the back stretch would be reduced to monotonous days and nights guarding against vandals and trespassers with only Frank, his fat partner for conversation. Between Frank's chomping on pizza and expelling it with gas, Monk would slowly go insane. He hoped Betsy could be convinced to continue their relationship if it might be called that. He feared the walls closing in, and he had no desire to be casted at an empty racecourse till the fall meet in November.

The romantic dinner he had planned remained a few hours away. He might cash a bet at the races before then. Jim McGarrah, a young trainer with a few decent horses had given him a tip yesterday. McGarrah's horse, Storm Strike was running in the Governor's Handicap. It was a tough race according to his analysis of the day's Racing Form, but McGarrah assured him that, barring any unforeseen traffic problems during the mile race, Storm Strike was fit enough to win. The security guard thought he had time to make a bet and watch the race from the grandstand. Watching a race might distract him enough to quit obsessing over the murder. It would help him stay sober definitely.

He couldn't afford to buy whiskey at the racetrack bar, bet on the race and go on a fancy dinner.

He didn't gamble with money as a rule, except for occasional small stakes card games to pass the time. Monk relegated gambling in his mind to bigger, more risky issues. The adrenaline payoff had to at least come close to combat for it to excite Monk. But he was willing to bet a twenty-dollar bill on the tip. If he won, it would mean the difference between cheap wine or expensive wine at dinner. He parked his old pickup near the guard shack and walked around the track for a half mile from the barn area to the front grandstand. The sun burned the back of his neck and sweat oozed from what seemed like every pore.

Monk felt exhausted by the time he reached the tunnel under the grandstand that led to the paddock where the horses for the race would be saddled. Too much drinking and smoking. Fuck, he wasn't even thirty-years-old. He promised himself that he would get back in shape once the meet closed and he had more spare time. He remembered running the obstacle course effortlessly during his Army days as he coughed and sputtered into the saddling area.

The crowd milled around like birds near the enclosed saddling area. They pecked at peanuts, drank over-priced beer from plastic cups, strutted, skipped, hopped, sauntered, and a few strode around the circled area with the pretend air of equine experts. Monk learned from the trainers and jockeys that real experts among gamblers were rare because thoroughbred horses, like people, ran hot and cold. Their temperament varied daily. Only a few could be measured with any sort of routine predictability. It was why racetracks made money and most gamblers stayed poor. Monk categorized the crowd based on their dress and manner. The peacocks pranced in brightly colored shirts and pants, the pigeons hung on the paddock fence hoping for a morsel of information, the crows hustled naïve bettors offering trips for the price of a pari-mutuel ticket, and the chickens clucked around in confused groups staring at programs and racing forms. The serious punters, the hawks, stood motionless and alert for signs from the horses before placing their bets—too much sweaty froth on a horse's neck indicated nervousness, up on the bit and pulling the groom around might indicate fitness and eagerness to run, a dull coat was a sign of health problems or bad care.

The horses all stood in their saddling stalls according to their numbers when the valets entered carrying saddles, numbered saddle cloths, and whips. It was a small field of five horses running for the Governor's Handicap and a purse of 100,000 dollars. The money provided a good incentive but stiffened the competition as well. The five trainers worked quickly, saddling horses, checking bridles, and removing protective bandages from valuable legs. The noise level rose outside the paddock as the crowd anticipated making their bets. The anxiety rose in the paddock as both horse and trainer sensed that everything in their lives came down to the next few minutes. Storm Strike looked ready nuzzling McGarrah playfully as the trainer checked the bridle for the third time. Five jockeys strolled around the corner from the jock's room and stood by the trainers, waiting for orders.

Dr. Steadmon, the state veterinarian walked by and examined each horse for unreported injury. The paddock judge followed close on her heels, raised each horse's upper lip to compare the tattoo numbers against the numbers on their registration papers, and called for each rider to mount. The trainers "legged up" their riders, and the grooms led the horses out of the paddock to the waiting ponies that would warm them up and guide them into the starting gate. Storm Strike pricked his ears and bucked once when the bugle player blew the call to the post.

Monk bought his ticket and a beer and headed into the grandstand to an empty box seat at the finish. The heat seemed to rise from the track surface with tiny hands. Its hot fingers of air pulled him down. He felt heavy and slow as he sipped his beer and the horses paraded by the crowd. McGarrah's horse pranced excitedly, his hooves barely touching the racetrack. That was a good sign, thought Monk. A couple of the jockeys waved at small children with their faces pressed against the fence as they squealed with delight. By the time the parade passed the grandstand and broke into a slow canter, the noise from the crowd had toned down to a slight hum inside the security guard's head along with any thoughts of Red Harvey.

Pulling up and reigning in around the five-furlong pole, the horses turned into the mile chute. The five horses, guided by their lead ponies, walked down the chute, and circled behind the starting gate. The official starter surveyed them all from his tower as his assistants took the horses away from the pony riders and loaded each one into the numbered metal cages. Peaceful Night went in smoothly. The assistant starter jumped on the metal framework and steadied the horse's head. The jockey riding him pulled his goggles down and readied for the break. Native Son entered followed by Storm Strike and Tiger Warrior. Sporting Chance fought with his handler and backed away from the gate. His jockey kicked the horse's flanks. Sporting Chance seemed very nervous and balked again. The stallion's shoulders were covered with thick white foam. Finally, the stallion loaded. They were all in position.

Storm Strike exploded in the starting gate. The well-seasoned gelding was not known for acting up act up in the gate before a race. As far as omens went this was a bad one, if you believed in omens. The jockey Fernandez stayed in the saddle and the assistant starter checked to make sure none of the horse's legs were injured or cut. But what worried Monk was the fact that whatever rattled Storm might prevent a good break. This was a huge animal with a voracious stride. According to the racing form, the horse ran his best on the front end, reaching out and eating up the track. The jockeys crouched low over the necks of their mounts. The horses all froze in expectation. The grandstand crowd stopped screaming. Then Storm Strike's handler yelled "okay" from inside the starting gate. The starter pressed the button. The bell rang, the electric doors sprang open, and the horses leaped away from the gate.

They broke evenly except for Storm Strike who got away very slowly, as Monk had feared. Even the late runner, Tiger Warrior, broke ahead of him. The track announcer called the race over the loudspeaker. The riders jockeyed for position as the racing field moved in a tangled ball of legs and tails toward the half-mile pole. Dirt flew from the horses' hooves, singing against plastic goggles, stinging the faces of the horses behind and beside them.

Sporting Chance went to the front and opened up two lengths on the rest of the field. Peaceful Night and Native Son ran neck and neck, inside and outside along the rail. Tiger Warrior hugged the rail three lengths behind them saving ground before the turn. Fernandez stood almost straight in the irons holding Storm Strike back and toward the middle of the track. Why the hell doesn't he give him his head, thought Monk? I bet his trainer, McGarrah, is pissed off. The horse can't run behind other horses. He needs the lead. Maybe Fernandez was worried because Storm broke so bad, thinking that by saving the horse on the backside there would be more run left down the stretch. The only problem with that lay in time and distance, like a jet airplane trying to take off on a short runway. Would the horse run out of ground before he could catch the leader?

As the field passed the half-mile pole and rounded the turn, Sporting Chance ran out of wind and began backing up. Peaceful Night and Native Son, still running together like a team of plow horses, rushed by him. The jockey on Native Son urged the horse slightly ahead of Peaceful Night, but still not asking him to run full out. Tiger Warrior gained ground along the rail and Storm Strike coasted dead last. Within a few seconds he knew the running order changed because he heard the crowd start screaming again and saw them stand. Native Son passed the tote board first. Peaceful Night faded fast. Tiger Warrior closed on the leader and just outside the final eighth pole caught him. It was a hell of a race but where was Storm Strike?

Manny Devereoux and Mark Sanders, the rider on Tiger Warrior, were locked in a duel. Devereoux hand rode Native Son. The old stallion wouldn't respond to the whip and so Manny stretched out along his thick neck, sliding the knotted reins up and down his mane with both hands in perfect cadence to the thrust of each hoof. It seemed to Monk as he watched that horse and rider were the same being, as if the motion of Manny's body lifted the massive stallion off the earth and gave him wings. Sanders was good too, really good. He had raised the whip in his left hand, cracked Tiger Warrior's ass at least six times in three strides, and driving him up, wedged the horse between Native Son and the rail. Each rider could have reached out and touched the other. You saw no daylight between horses. It looked like a magnificent finish when the crowd rose to its feet again, clapping wildly and chanting *Storm Strike- Storm Strike-Storm Strike.* A huge, dark blur shot by at the far end of the tote board.

Fernandez and the gelding flew down the middle of the track unnoticed by the other two riders. Devereoux and Sanders might as well have had their mounts tethered to a furlong pole. Storm Strike caught them about a hundred feet from the wire. In one jump Storm was even with them and still accelerating when they all finished with the flash of the automatic camera.

Everything happened so fast Monk wasn't even sure that what he had seen was real. Maybe he was dreaming. No horse could run the last eighth of a mile of any race that quickly. The jockeys stood in the irons, leaning back on the reins to slow their horses down. Moving at a full gallop, the pony boy caught Fernandez and Storm strike midway down the backside of the track. Storm Strike snorted and shook his head, trying to dodge the boy's hand when he reached for the D on the bit to pass the leather lead line through it. The horse wasn't finished running. The boy missed the first time, but made the exchange on the second and reined Storm in. Jose Fernandez gave him control of the horse's head, fell back in the saddle and loosened his hold on the reins. All the jockeys were completely out of breath. Their chests heaved and shuddered as they sucked hot air into their lungs.

When the field of horses returned to the front of the grandstand, the tote board flashed *Photo...Photo...Photo* and the order of finish lights, which had Storm Strike unofficially first, Native Son second, and Tiger Warrior third, flickered off and on. The track announcer informed the bettors over the PA system, "Please hold all para-mutuel wagering tickets while the stewards examine the photograph." The officials would have to judge the exact placement of horses before a winner could be declared and bets paid off. Certainly, it was too close to call with the naked eye. The two horses that finished up the track were already on the way back to the barn area and the first three paced around the winner's circle with their riders still in the saddle.

The crowd grew restless. After what seemed an hour, but was only a couple of minutes, the lights on the tote board flashed once more and then stopped. The word *Official* lit up next to the three numbers, but the order had been reversed. Monk couldn't believe his eyes. Tiger Warrior finished first, then Native Son, and then Storm Strike. Even though the big gelding had been the freshest horse in the race at the end, he started his run too late to catch the other horses. The invisible line, or wire, that ran across the track created the illusion of being straight. It was, in point of fact, angled to make the distance equal between the outside and inside rails. The photo posted by the judges clearly indicated Tiger Warrior crossing first by a short nose. But the distance separating all three was less than a foot and two strides beyond the wire found Storm a good half a length in front. The crowd voiced their disappointment, booing the tote board as if it were alive and somehow made the decision. Storm Strike went off prohibitive favorite, meaning a lot of money was lost including Monk's twenty dollars.

Monk thought about Phelps laughing at him when he brought up the matter of justice in their conversation as if the word was a joke. He considered the fact that Storm Strike, the obvious best horse in this race ended up third by a matter of inches and realized why Phelps laughed. What we hope will happen does happen on occasion but randomly. What we hope will happen so rarely does because our expectation creates a bias not based on reality. Justice is nothing more than a fair and reasonable outcome in each situation. It doesn't happen in war when the guy next to you gets his shit blown away by a grenade and you don't get a scratch. You experience the lack of it in nature when the nicest people in the world have everything they own destroyed by a tornado or a family member cut down by cancer. In law enforcement, justice is a joke. Criminals get off on technicalities, innocent people go to jail, and corruption is a way of life. It was a cynical outlook, but one Monk understood how Joe Phelps could make it his world view. Was he, Monk, hoping for a better outcome in Red's case, like in this race? Yes. However, was the idea of justice for the old hardboot race tracker not only out of Monk's control but outside the boundaries of reality as well?

Headline: Study Proves Drinking Like a Fish Healthy Only If You Drink What a Fish Does

"Talking about personal stuff makes me pretty damn uncomfortable," said Monk.

"Then you need to understand why we are doing it," Betsy answered.

Monk's plans for a romantic dinner with Betsy seemed to be ending up in the scree of his life. He had saved a week's pay for this night at Pat's Steakhouse. The restaurant opened less than a year ago over on Brownsboro Road and quickly became the go-to spot for movers and shakers in various political and corporate positions. The prices for steaks reflected that. He even put a tie on, his only one, so they could get through the door. But he saw trouble coming when he picked Betsy up from J.C.'s for their 7PM reservation. She was dressed in jeans and a black Grateful Dead tee-shirt. He asked her why, and she replied that something deeply personal needed to be discussed.

"It's because I need to make you understand that I think you're important enough for me to tell you some things. What you think of me matters to me."

He found himself close beside her in the cab of his pickup truck, forcing the anxiety into the corner of his mind reserved for unpleasant necessities, the kind he hated to face but disciplined himself to do, like paying the electric bill or working while sober. The truck was idling with a soft growl and the green lights glowed from the instrument panel. The electric transformer above the bar hummed, and the street smelled of stale beer and exhaust fumes. There were no stars, only a sliver of a moon, and the few streetlights were a dirty yellow. He was surrounded by shadows in his mind and in the dark night.

"What you think of me matters to me," she repeated, her voice faltering slightly. "Even though we barely know each, I feel like what happens from here on is important to us both. I'm no prize, Monk, and I'm no virgin. You should know that by now. I'm my own person. But I fell in love once before. So, even the remote possibility that I'm heading that way again terrifies me. I have to put the brakes on."

"Who was he?"

"He drove stock cars on the dirt track circuit. A bad wreck crippled him. I was very young and wasn't strong enough to stay with him when he needed me to help him heal. I regret that."

Monk shook his head. An expression of disgust wrinkled his smooth, tanned face. His left eye began twitching.

"Poor Betsy. You must be a good Catholic girl and I must be your penance." He lit a cigarette and inhaled deeply. The smoke punctuated each word. "You couldn't do right by a physical cripple, so you find a guy you think is emotionally damaged to atone for your sins. They're different things. Me and your ex-boyfriend aren't the same, although I do think of war as a car wreck sometimes. But I can't redo what I've done any more than he can. That's one of the great flaws in our humanity. People can't be fixed."

"Is that what you think? You're a fucking idiot, Monk. I'm simply hoping you can understand that you're not in this thing we call life by yourself. Nobody lives in a vacuum, including you. We've all made mistakes. Quit feeling so damn sorry for yourself. This isn't all about you. I think there's something here between us, and I need to stop it now before we both end up in a mess. So, I need tell you something I should have told you when we first met. He's not my ex-boyfriend. We're married, and my husband is a cripple, yes. Maybe I expected too much from him and myself at the time, but I do love him in my own way. He's asked me to come back to him, to try and work out if there's any reason for us to stay married. It's been almost two years since I ran. I'm a weak person. I know that, but I feel very deeply that I need to bring him and me some closure. I won't be able to live with myself if I don't much less anybody else. I'm leaving for Texas in two days. I'm sorry. I hate to spring this on you so quickly and unexpectedly. He and I spent three hours on the phone this morning. I'm sorry because I really do have feelings for you too. I need to do this, or I'll hate myself worse than I already do. I honestly don't know how things will turn out."

She sobbed and moved to hug him. He held her back, a little shocked and angry but unable to voice it because, like love, all his emotions were exercises that issued from his conscious mind rather than true and from the heart. He knew these were only thoughts about the way he was supposed to feel, but he couldn't seem to repair the brokenness that made him this way. It was an infirmity he brought home from war. He buried all feeling to survive Vietnam, and his spectrum of moods had atrophied. He had struggled to generate a true feeling for Betsy, no matter how vague, and he almost got there. Now, he realized warm twinge in his mind was simply a reaction that he should sense something, anything.

She closed the truck door softly and hurried away without giving him a chance to respond, although he wasn't sure what he might say. The episode had surprised him more than anything. All he could conjure up seemed to be the strong desire for bourbon, and he knew the perfect place. Slamming the truck into first gear, he squealed away from the curb. The night folded over him and darkness consumed him as quickly as the excitement of being in something that might have been love disappeared.

***

An imitation Irish Pub spread over the second floor of Pat's like an oasis in the formal atmosphere of the downstairs dining area. Still wearing his tie and with a pocket full of money, Monk settled for an evening alone and a dinner of Old Forester, his favorite top shelf, but usually unaffordable, bourbon. The place sang with a small, but lively, crowd of smiling drunks. Two women dressed in expensive cocktail dresses and an inordinate amount of shiny jewelry graced the mahogany bar. They were attractive and surrounded by five men aggressively vying for their attention. An Irish jig danced in the air from speakers above the bar. Normally, he would have surveyed the room sitting with his back to the wall, a habit called situational awareness developed as a survival technique. But he was no longer at war, and he didn't much care about surviving now. He sat on a stool at the opposite end of the others and nodded at the bartender, an oily fellow in a short-sleeve white shirt and black bowtie with a smile too large to be sincere.

"What can I get you, Sir.?"

"Old Forester, neat. Start me a tab."

The bartender tuned his back and reached for a bottle on an upper shelf. He poured a liberal shot in a lowball glass with no ice and sat it in front of Monk on a coaster. The amber liquid went down smoothly. He normally drank Old Crow or Jim Beam. Both had an aftertaste like kerosene and a made your head feel caught in a vice the next day. But they were cheap and so was the security company that paid him. Old Forester had a much better flavor. You could taste some honey and caramel, maybe even a little fruit on your tongue. The trick to this lay in patience. You had to let the bourbon air for a few seconds in the glass and let the harsh smell of fingernail polish dissipate first. Monk was not long-suffering on this night, however, and drank three shots rapidly. He ordered another shot when a new couple arrived on the landing at the head of the stairs.

The man was recognizable immediately. The gubernatorially candidate and accused fraud, Whitney Landis, strode into the bar area with a beautiful, but vacuous looking blonde attached to his wrist and bouncing along like she was a balloon filled with helium. They found a dark corner with an empty table and sat so close to each other that it might have been the same chair. Obviously too young and not sour enough to be a politician's wife, she must have been one of his interns or a hooker, or both. That fucking snake is getting lucky tonight, thought Monk. He had no use for Landis and had even entertained the idea that Landis' bodyguard might have been the one who put the beat down on Red Harvey because of Red's grand jury testimony upcoming in the racehorse ringer scandal. Joe Phelps checked it out, though, and they both alibied out. Still, rich and entitled people angered him. Politicians nauseated him. Landis was both. The sight of Landis caused his stomach to roll and he felt his cheeks flush what must have been a bright red.

Two more shots of bourbon and the continuing giggles of Landis and his blonde sent Monk into a funk of despair that rolled quickly into a ball of rage. He wasn't sure why the anger in him kept rising in his throat. Maybe it had to do with Betsy and another failure at attempting a real relationship with another human, or maybe the bullet in Red Harvey's brain nagged at his thoughts. Maybe it was the memory of a bad war, or just life in general. All he knew for sure was that he had had too much whiskey in too short a time. No one had ever accused him of good judgment. He paid his tab, gave the bartender a tip, and turned to leave. The bartender offered to call a cab, which Monk refused adamantly. A man, even drunk, took himself home. A man controlled his own life. The room spun as he stumbled from the bar stool.

He got to the entrance, almost. In the back of his mind the word don't-don't-don't flashed it neon colors. It was that little voice of good judgment that the alcohol had muted and it popped up at the precise moment he saw Whitney's blonde companion excuse herself from his table. She headed toward the lady's room and Monk could not force his body to not turn around completely from the doorway. As if controlled by an itch that had to be scratched or he would go insane, he approached

Landis who looked at him without the slightest bit of recognition or concern.

"You're an asshole and a criminal," Monk said.

"An astute observation if you knew me or my business."

"I know your type. You think you can do whatever you want whenever you want to whoever you want."

"It's whom."

Landis spoke and a smirk spread slowly across his face. In an supreme effort of self-control, Monk refrained from shoving his balled fist into the condescending smile.

"I know your game and I still believe it's connected to Red Harvey's death."

"Who's Red Harvey?"

"He's a nobody, just like I'm a nobody." Monk began slurring his words slightly as the bourbon saturated his brain. "But he knew what I know. The mare you bred to Big Spruce had twins. They both lived. You placed one with a cheap old broodmare and sold the other for a lot of money. Then you forged registration papers and ran the one you kept in a cheap claiming race. You made a fortune somehow when it won, and Red ended up dead in an alley."

"You certainly have a vivid imagination, and you give me a lot of credit. No one is lucky or smart enough to go through the process you described successfully. Ringers in horseracing are a myth. You're boring me. Go away before I have the bartender call security and throw you out."

Landis laughed as the woman came back to the table. She looked frightened as if Monk might know Whitney's wife.

"Is everything okay?" She asked.

"Mr. Whatever-your-name-is has just explained a movie plot to me. It's a fantasy."

That quickly, the scene ended. Her voice shattered any composure Monk might have had. Taking two steps backward, he mumbled, "This isn't over." Landis dismissed him with a wave. He spun around almost falling over and stumbled out the entrance. Navigating the steps carefully with both hands on the rail, he descended the flight of stairs and pushed the front door open thinking about how easy it was to embarrass yourself when drinking good bourbon.

The humid night hung over the parking lot like a wet wool blanket. The summer had yet to fully arrive, but there were only two seasons in Louisville, Kentucky, really. Hot and cold. Sweat poured from Monk's body. His white shirt got soaked before he reached the pickup truck. Stopping to feel a slight breeze, stare upward at the stars, and still the spinning of the earth around him, he noticed a tiny red glow in the corner of his left eye. Turning numbly to survey the source, Monk saw the shadowed outline of a man under one of the dim night lights. The man leaned on the trunk of a dark, Lincoln town car and continued smoking but never looked away from him. Monk turned to face his stare and took three steps toward the man.

"See something funny?"

"Just a drunk guy trying to find his ride."

The man continued lounging in a relaxed position and did not seem to be menaced in the slightest by Monk's approach. The slack face from which the voice escaped came into focus, an ugly face in a handsome, chiseled way. Monk chuckled to himself as he approached the figure. Oh hell, the night just kept getting better. When the man stood up from leaning on the car, he rose to well over six feet and looked about thirty pounds of lean muscle heavier than Monk. The face was instantly recognizable by the oblong-shaped head with a round chin and aquiline nose that altogether presented an incongruent image of Mr. Potato Head with short blond hair. The closer Monk, the more the man's dead eyes protruded like a frog's. He recognized the man as Robert Franklin Goss, Landis' bodyguard, even though he had never met him and had seen him only once.

"What's on your mind?"

"Your master, the next corrupt governor, ever let you off the leash?"

"I'm going to excuse your manners since you're obviously drunk."

"And I'm going to excuse your face since you had no choice in its formation."

Whitney Landis' bodyguard became visibly irritated, taking a long step toward Monk who exploded a left jab into the man's face without even thinking about what a bad move the punch was in his condition. He could barely stand. The man's head rocked back slightly. His body, in a solidly braced posture with legs shoulder-width apart and right foot in front of the left, like a modified Weaver pistol-shooting stance, never moved. Monk raised a right hook, but it never reached the mark. Goss whirled one hundred and eighty degrees and stepped his back into Monk's body. His right arm shot straight up, blocking the right hook on his forearm. Then he dropped the right elbow hard into Monk's solar plexus and before Monk's breath even escaped in a painful whine, the bodyguard brought the arm up like a lever and hit Monk with a back-handed fist square on the nose. It was a common self-defense move that every ex-military guy, including Monk, knew. Blood spurted out of his nose as he dropped to his knees puking all over Goss' shiny wing-tipped shoes.

Headline: Drunk Finds Clarity While Nursing Bruised Hangover

Having no recollection how he had gotten into his truck, much less how he drove it all the way to the racetrack or what guard working night shift had let him through the gate, a sore and severely hungover Monk Johnson pried open his puffy eyes and at first could see nothing but the swollen sides of his nose. His nose had swelled enough to almost block his vision. When he reached to touch it, it felt like a soft and rotted peach had been stuck to his face. But the pain made him withdraw his fingers quickly.

As the rest of the world came into blurry focus, he found himself parked close to the entrance at the track kitchen, which was open for business. That meant it had to be at least 5 AM. A few horsemen stopped by the truck, shook their heads, and laughed. Monk gave them a middle finger. Most ignored him. A hungover drunk beaten to a bloody pulp and sleeping in his vehicle happened to be an ordinary sight on Sunday mornings after the Louisville bars had closed from a rowdy Saturday night, especially during the race meet. Many of the racing stables came from Chicago or around Lexington, Kentucky. Some big-time New York stables always left a few horses after the Derby to help fill races and keep the racing secretary happy so they could be assigned choice barns the following year. But since Swaps shipped in from California and won the 1955 Kentucky Derby, stables from the West operated by pretend cowboys had begun filtering in. Competing and winning races in the state of Kentucky, which housed the most famous breeding farms and produced the best runners, added prestige to the trainers who ran these stables, and a good reputation meant new clients, more money. The cowboys who worked for those west coast trainers always tried to live up to their myth. From the last week of April through the month of June, Saturday nights often brought the wild west to Kentucky. The battered security guard liked details that popped into his mind often and at very odd times. They gave him perspective. Usually, Monk didn't mind the cowboys unless forced into the role of referee on the backside. It created too much opportunity for him to get injured breaking up a fight. On this day, however, it might provide an excuse for his appearance.

His punching bag of a face embarrassed him, and he knew ridicule would come upon entry into the kitchen, but the need for coffee and a piece of toast to calm his bucking horse stomach overrode his self-consciousness. Surprisingly, the jokes were minimal as most of the attention gathered on Salvation Sally, who stood on a chair and railed against an incomprehensible evil of some kind and the end of the world along with it. Monk struggled and reached for a small portion of pity toward the woman. Some of her congregation seemed to believe and others chuckled at the insanity, but like watching any disaster unfold, no one could turn away.

Most of the crowd consisted of decent folk. He knew them enough to say hello at least. They were the lowest workers on the racetrack social and economic scale, hotwalkers, grooms, stable boys, exercise riders slightly too heavy to ever be jockeys. They had no other place to be. This was home. True, some were drunks, some runaways, many itinerants, but very few would ever be guilty of crimes that went against their gypsy-like code of honor. Protect the horses in your care. Be loyal to your clan, which was the stable you worked for. Don't steal from friends. Be willing to fight if disrespected and share material things with those who have less. They held strong beliefs in superstitions and traditions, especially luck and fate. That's why Salvation Sally could draw a big enough crowd when preaching to earn a meager living. Well, that and the fact that she offered rewards for small donations to her ministry work at a set rate—three dollars for a hand job, five for a blowjob, and ten for around the world. And she wasn't bad looking in a used sort of way, a little dirty and unkempt with faded jeans and a dull glaze over what used to be blue eyes, Sally's features were still crisp and elegant like a porcelain cup stained by hard service.

Monk felt no moral judgment or distaste toward her. First because he thought sex should never have been classified as sin and second because somewhere in her damaged and demented self a clean soul existed that made her actions holy. He wished his mind had that much innocent freedom. Listening to the end of her sermon as he nursed a cup of black coffee and stared at his uneaten piece of toast searching for a seed of logic, maybe even hope, he found neither.

"And when he had opened the third seal I heard the third beast sayCome and seeAnd I beheldandlowablackhorseand the jockey that sat on him had a pair of scales in his hand. And I heard avoice in the midst of the four beasts say, A measure of wheat for a penny, and three measures of barley for a penny; and *see* thou hurt not the oil and the wine. You must make the weight or be disqualifiedHewho can't make the weight can't ride. Jezebel Jezebel why have you forsaken me. Is this an olive garden. Let's see, no its Gethsemane Paraazz Gawd and donate Paraazz Jaysus and get yore reward And Jesus went out and departed from the temple and his disciples came to him for to she whim the buildings of the temple And Jesus said unto them, Seeye not all these things? verily I say unto you, There shall not be left here one stone upon another that shall not be thrown down And as he sat upon his Jar of Olives, the disciples came unto him privately, saying, Tell us, when shall these things be and what shall be the sign of thy coming, and of the end of the world And Jesus answered and said unto them Take heed that no man deceive you For many shall come in my name, saying I am Christ and shall deceive many But I ain't no con man Who has grew up before him like a tender shootandlikearootoutofdryground. He had no beauty or majesty to attract us but he accepted donations and so will I. PARRAAZZ GAWD."

The rant ended and the small crowd dissipated in silence. It might have been reverence for some, confusion for others, but Monk thought that much of the crowd may have been wondering how this woman remained out of Central State Hospital on the outskirts of Louisville. At least, he wondered that himself and realized that the isolated and secured backside of the racetrack protected her from the world around them.

A young man, maybe in his late teens or early twenties, approached the table where Salvation Sally stood. Her eyes were closed, and she listed left and then right, swaying like a metronome on the tabletop until he reached out and touched her leg. Mumbling incoherently, Sally extended a hand, which the young man folded gently into his own. He helped her step from the table to a chair and finally the floor. Steadying her, the man whispered something in her ear, and she nodded. He turned abruptly and left the track kitchen. Sally followed closely but stopped as she passed Monk's table.

"I can heal your face from its sins," she said. "The pain will go away washed by the blood of the Lamb."

"Thanks, but this face saw enough blood last night. I'll pass."

"May I speak to you of blasphemy, brother Monk."

"I'd rather you didn't."

"It has to do with your job as protector of us backside sinners."

As bad as he felt, Monk was also intrigued. He pulled a chair out indicating that she take a seat. He had swallowed two Canadian aspirins earlier. They were illegal because the pills also contained a healthy dose of codeine. The old fellow who ran the tack trailer selling horse supplies next to the kitchen got a few bottles whenever a stable shipped down from Canada. The trainers sometimes used them for certain injuries to their horses, especially if they were being rested and not subject to race day blood tests, but they were also useful for human injuries and hangovers, both plentiful on the backside. Monk's headache was slipping into memory.

"I saw the sign of the devil, and I was afraid," she said as her eyes widened.

"Where did you see this sign, Sally."

"I was on my knees in a feed shed praising the Lord and giving old fat Hoss his reward for a donation. He seemed very thankful for his blessing. Moaning so loud in tongues as the Holy Spirit surge through him, and I was so happy in the Lord myself that neither of us noticed that little devil sneak into the feed room."

"When was this?"

"A few days ago at breakfast time for the horses when the barn was pretty much empty."

"What happened?"

Sally stared upward at the grease spattered ceiling over the kitchen grill. Her gaze circled the room and settled on a table where Hoss, Victor, Rueben Garcia, and Willy Simmons played poker for pennies, each one hoping to earn enough change for a bottle of Mad Dog 20/20 that would help the winner pass the afternoon in paradise. She began to tremble all over and rolled her eyes back in her head as if a seizure might be coming. Monk covered her shaky hand with his own shaky hand. Touching her made him uncomfortable. It was way too intimate a gesture, but he couldn't seem to stop himself.

"I seen the sign of the Devil. He showed it to me when he dropped his pants. I got so scared I jumped up and ran away before old Hoss finished getting his reward. I hope Jesus forgave me 'cause I didn't return the five dollars."

"What did you see, Sally? What did you see?"

"The Devil's eyeball staring straight at me. Big, it was big and round and blue in the middle below the belly button Eve gave Adam's offspring after they got cast from the Garden for eating apples. The Devil was crying, crying one big tear because I was working for Jesus instead of him. He tried to force his human body on me. I fought the urges coming from it. I fought my fear and prayed and then, I ran."

Salvation Sally's eyes welled up and tear formed in the corners. She struggled to keep her voice low and refused to look anywhere but at Monk. He didn't want to press the issue further. She seemed on the verge of hysteria but not quite there, just balanced on the edge of a cliff of sanity so precariously that a slight wind would blow her into the abyss. He couldn't stop himself. The eyeball image instantly reminded him of the conversation during his poker game a few evenings before. It seemed incredible that Sally had seen a killer with the same tattoo, but even more incredible that two men had the same unique tattoo in the exact same place on their bodies.

"Tell me the name of the man, Sally, and I'll protect you from him and the Devil both."

She dropped her head and stared at the tabletop answering him with a whisper.

"It was Victor. Lord Jesus, Victor's got the Devil in him."

Headline: Cosmic Karma Exists

The bare nail frightened Victor. Short hairs on the back of his head rose as if an electric current had passed over them and his stomach jumped as if he had seen his grandma rise from her grave. He stared at the nail. The single bare spike of steel on a tack room wall covered with bridles, bits, racing silks, blinkers, leather lead shanks and girth pads made him realize his aloneness. He knew every piece of racing equipment that hung on the wall, where it came from, what it fit, how much it cost. But all of sudden, he couldn't remember what should be hanging on the empty nail, only that *something* should be.

The fear grew quickly. Victor was no mystic. He knew nothing of other worlds, parallel realities, ghosts, demons, gods, or goblins. He understood very little about time, how it really travelled or where it came from. He knew only the base things of life. If he was hungry, he ate. If he had to piss, he did. When an itch came, Victor scratched it. He drank all the time for the express purpose of not thinking. That was his life, and he accepted it. But in this instant, his universe was out of order. Once before at this spring Churchill Downs race meeting a dread like this had entered the pit of his stomach and loosened his bowels. A.J. had entered one of Victor's favorite horses in a cheap claiming race and when the race came up, the rain came down. It poured and poured. The track turned to soup on the surface and that allowed the horses hooves to sink all the way to the bedrock beneath. When they ran, it sounded like a machine gun firing against a concrete wall.

Barbizon Beau, the horse was named Barbizon Beau. He was small and pigeon-toed, his front hooves turned in so bad you thought the legs might be on backwards. But he could run and he had some heart. He never gave up and he had made the stable a little money over a couple of racing seasons. The problem was—and this is what Victor tried to explain to his boss A.J. Barbizon Beau could barely stand up on a wet track. A. J. knew that and told Victor to shut his pie hole. He was the trainer, not Victor who couldn't even wipe his ass unless he was drunk. That's when this terrible feeling nested like snakes in his gut. Sometimes you just know things are not going to turn out good. You didn't have to be smart to know that.

God damn A.J. should have listened. Beau took four jumps out of the starting gate, lost his traction, and fell. When they got the old boy to finally stand up, his left front ankle just dangled from the canon bone like a wallowed-out ball joint bearing on a piece of worn machinery. They only had one choice, which was no choice at all. The state veterinarian dropped him with a hot shot right on the spot and the tractor hauled his carcass off the racecourse to whatever hell good racehorses went to.

Victor didn't know why that same feeling was back. It wasn't even cloudy, much less raining, and they had no horses running on this day. The feeling had come over him in the track kitchen this very morning. Salvation Sally huddled close to that security guard who always poked his nose in everybody's business, Monk Johnson. They both stared at him. He felt their eyes burning a hole in his chest. Why? Did Sally know about Red Harvey? Red Harvey had stuck his nose in the wrong place, too. He had gone through Victor's one old suitcase under his cot in the tack room looking for vodka and found that fucking gun. Victor never really hid the thing because no one ever went through his stinking dirty clothes. He had nothing to steal just like the rest of his buddies. But Red found it in a sock while he was looking for vodka, just a little thing Victor had stolen from his grandma years ago.

It wasn't a big problem till Red made it one and tried to blackmail him. They was at Freddy's and Red was broke. He told Victor to give him some money for a drink or he'd report that gun to Monk Johnson. That do-gooder fake cop would've taken it away, and the stewards would've ruled him off the track for having it. Victor would be left homeless, no money, no job, no whiskey. Damn, he sure needed some whiskey right now. Besides, that gun had been useful for other things. Things that quieted Victor's brain, things that kept him from being disrespected by low class women. He needed it in case the urge to teach some more bad women a lesson overcame him.

When Victor followed Red out of Freddy's bar, he was going to try and make a deal with Red to keep him quiet. That's all. Keep him quiet. Fucking Butch Chernov came running at Red with a goddamn ball bat and thumped the old boy real good with it. Red went down like a sack of potatoes and laid there. Chernov ran off and Red sat back up, bleeding and staring off into the distance like a stunned old cow at the slaughterhouse. What did it hurt with no one else around to squeeze one off behind Red's ear? The little gun didn't make much noise. It sounded like a tab top on a beer can being pulled open. If the old boy was probably going to die anyway, it didn't matter. If he wasn't, it guaranteed his mouth stayed shut. Like buying an exacta ticket both ways. You boxed the numbers, and no matter which horse ran first and which one second, you still became a winner. It was a sure thing. He might have hated putting a bullet in Red's brain pan except for one thing. Red was a friend, but Victor didn't like Red more than he liked Victor. You got to look out for number one first. But what if Red had told Sally about the gun when he was getting a reward? He had to ditch that gun. People were staring at him all the way back to the barn when he left the track kitchen. He hated people staring at him.

Something grazed Victor's left leg as if a small hand brushed lint from his pants. He tried to stand up from his seat on the edge of the cot, but the movement took his breath away and caused great pain. Dizzy, he fell back on his cot. What touched him? He had to know.

The crazy calico barn cat jumped onto the cot and sprawled across Victor's chest. He looked into its eyes and saw nothing but his own reflection. "Get off me. Get off I say." The cat licked a paw and stared straight ahead. He had seen that vacant gaze before. Where? Where had he seen it? The image of his grandma's face crossed his mind. The old bitch laid in bed the morning before he'd run away so many years ago and spoke through a box that looked like an electric razor held tightly against her throat. The words came out like they were coated with helium. "Too much gin and too many Camels. I ain't the same since they cut out my voice box and the cataract took my left eye. Won't be around much longer, but my good eye will always be on you. You keep your hand off your little dickie bird when I'm gone. Nothing good comes from that thing. I'll be watching." When she stared, it wasn't at Victor. It was through him. That one single eye burned a hole in his stomach.

The cat's gaze held the same dazed emptiness. Sadness consumed him like the morning fog that came off the Ohio River. It was empty. You could grab it but not hold onto it. The only reason you knew it was there was because you could see the outline of other things in its mist, things he had done to keep his dickie bird from evil when the urges came upon him. He felt no guilt about shooting those women, just a strange and heavy sense of dread in his chest. He was just trying to end the confusion he didn't understand that crowded into his brain when he thought of his grandma and those women on their knees. He wanted them there, but he didn't want them there. Victor shuddered. The cat leapt off his chest and onto the floor. An enormous weight lifted, carrying the sharp pain in his arm away. The sick feeling dangled at the top of his stomach and he wanted to scream out. All he could do was gasp for air and wipe the cold salt water from his cheek.

"Victor, get your lazy ass off that cot and bring me that cup of molasses to mix with the evening feed," A.J. stuck his head in the shadowed tack room and yelled, "I don't want to forget it later."

Now, he realized the bare nail had held the tin cup he used for the molasses keg. He held it in his hand. Slowly, the world came into focus around him. He walked the length of the barn and placed the cup on the ledge near his boss who was mixing a huge tub of oats with vitamins, bran, some corn, and a few other secret ingredients with hot water. A.J. upended the cup and the black, sweet, liquid dripped slowly into the tub. The concoction would steam under a burlap cover for a while, and then Victor and Hoss would feed it to each of the racehorses for their evening meal. A.J. called it a "mash," but Victor didn't know why.

"You've got about thirty minutes while this cooks up. Go find something to do."

A nap. A nap would be nice. He felt very tired. His mind drifted as he lay back down on his cot. The sun sank behind his eyes and life was perfect. He thought he heard the last race of the afternoon roar out of the gate, which had been placed at the six-furlong pole directly in front of A.J.'s barn on the backstretch. Victor saw a blur of colors, heard the bell, the jockeys chirping, and the crack of whips. He hung the pitchfork on its nails, stood the empty wheelbarrow against the barn wall, and sat down to watch the finish. He felt the ground shake beneath him. The slight smell of liniment and the excitement in his chest as the horses raced by made him wish he had a beer. His left arm tingled, and he leaned back in the lawn chair to rest for a minute. The loudspeaker blared out the names of the winner in the race. He heard Barbizon Beau, but static and a slight hum followed. The heat rustled in waves across the track like cellophane. The sweat, heavy on his eyelids, pulled them down like window blinds. Inside the room behind the window blinds, his mind walked around the barn one last time.

Headline: The Last Race of the Day

Life must be a race that no one wins. That was the thought that seemed stuck in Monk's mind as Churchill Down's closed its spring race meet for 1973. Much of the backside at the track rested in a somnambulant silence. Many of the horsemen and had shipped their stables to other tracks for the long hot summer—Ellis Park, Arlington, Fairgrounds, Calder. The wealthy stables headed east and west to Belmont, Aqueduct, Delmar, and Santa Anita. Other stables would soon follow. Churchill reopened in November for a short Fall Meet.

A few members of the maintenance crew repainted barns and the grounds keeper harrowed and dragged the sandy track to keep it safe for the few horses left to train. The track kitchen closed its doors immediately after lunch now. Even the muck pits were empty after the mushroom farmers swooped in with their trucks and loaded all the horseshit and straw to cover and fertilize their mushroom beds. Monk never ate mushrooms for this reason. They were grown in horseshit.

A racing circuit never ends, it follows a circle from beginning to end and begins again. The security guard hated himself for being philosophical, but maybe his reflections on the past few weeks were keeping him sane.

Monk sat on a hay bale stacked outside Ray Smithers' barn. He was out of breath. He lit a smoke and inhaled deeply, coughing and sputtering like a car engine that was running out of gas up a hill. His vision began to blur and then he realized it wasn't his vision, it was the world around him. Dusk, the shadow time, the space between light and dark when life was smoke and mirrors, when nothing held substance. Maybe this had led to the knot in his stomach. He had read somewhere Native Americans believed that during this limbo between day and night a shadow called a Wendigo could come out of its hiding place inside you and overtake your soul. Then, a man became a mere living shell, a form devoid of any essence. There were many things that could make a man empty, a bad love affair, a war like the one he had fought, being poor, being a junkie. Yet, all these things came to you from the outside and involved other people. Shadows came from within you. Every man cast his own shadow and, in his shadow, carried a dread of self.

In a sort of cosmic irony Victor and Red Harvey were buried side by side during a fifteen-minute service at Meadow Hill Cemetery in Jefferson County, Kentucky, which was already full of the homeless and the poor. The county paid the tab. The track Chaplin read a few useless words and a couple of old drunks threw some dirt on each pine box. Eleven people bowed their heads and Salvation Sally said a moving prayer for Red, but no one spoke for Victor. The whole service seemed to be an homage to injustice. It was certainly an end to a story that had no redeeming qualities for Monk.

On the Sunday of his conversation with Sally, he had rushed from the track kitchen along the main asphalt path past the clocker's stand, the gated gap that led from the barn area onto the track, the bleachers, and the newly erected game room for the workers that the Horsemen's Benevolent and Protective Association had paid for with the dues it collected. He turned left at the six-furlong pole and walked into A.J. Clark's barn with the idea of confronting Victor and catching him off guard. If what he surmised to be true was true in fact, then a gun would probably turn up somewhere among Victor's meager belongings. Victor would never throw away any item he could pawn for drinking money, even if it implicated him in murder. The little fellow just wasn't focused enough to think ahead past a bottle.

When he saw A.J. in the doorway of the tack room, the stricken look on the trainer's face alerted Monk immediately. A.J. stepped aside and Victor' body sat in peaceful response in an old lawn chair propped against the barn wall as if he had passed on with a clean conscience, or none at all. Joe Phelps was phoned and reluctantly showed up at Monk's insistence even though it was a Sunday. Among the bridles and saddles and medicines and blankets that decorated the old boy's home in the tack room, Phelps found a .22 caliber handgun that he called "a barkeep special." The track ambulance drove around and the EMT's loaded Victor up for his ride to the morgue. Although Victor had been young, his excessively indulgent lifestyle made him unhealthy. A.J. told Hoss to disinfect the room with Pine Sol. Hoss did and then got really drunk. By the next morning, Churchill Downs had returned to normal.

The following week, Jerome shared the coroner's report at their poker game. Victor died of a massive heart attack at the age of forty-three. The guy did, in fact, have a tearful eyeball tattooed in vivid colors just below his navel. There were no relatives found anywhere in the racetrack employment records or a home address. His emergency contacts listed—Red Harvey and Hoss Cartwright. Phelps gathered enough circumstantial evidence between the gun, the tattoo, the timing, and locations to believe Victor had killed the hookers and severely wounded the one, even though her brain had been too rattled to remember Victor's face. The bullet in Red's brain remained inexplicably. However, the probabilities led Phelps to close his cases as solved. What no one could answer and what stuck with Monk, the security guard, as the most important aspect of all these events was the single word most important in every language known to man, the most fundamental question in understanding, not only human behavior, but accepting the fluid motion of life. Why? Monk would never know for sure what drove Victor to commit his crimes and the not knowing caused him many sleepless nights. This was more out of curiosity than concern. But he began to understand a little more about what drove him, Monk Johnson, to worry about it at all. If his life was to be anything other than a restless and useless existence it would hinge on a search for the answer to that question in all things and always—why.

Perhaps in an effort to balance the natural world a little fate caught up with Whitney Landis. Joe Phelps called Monk two days after the funerals. Louisville vice cops had raided Evie Coomer's home with a search warrant. They found cash and betting slips under the bed and stuffed and sewn into the mattress. Also in the mattress, they found a log book directly related to Elvie's dealings, including the tattoo number of a race horse— *Z59324*—that was stabled with Jack Becker at Churchill and that had won a race early in the meet. The figures listed after the numbers indicated that Elvie took a considerable amount of money from Landis, laid it off with several big bookmakers in Las Vegas, St. Louis, Chicago, and Newark. The illegal return on the bets was over half a million dollars.

Vice turned the tattoo numbers over to the state racing commission, and they discovered the horse was owned by Whitney Landis. Maybe some slight notion of justice would be coming out of this whole deal, thought Monk, if not for Red specifically and the dead hookers, at least for the universe at large. The stewards would soon discover what Monk already believed. The horse was a ringer, maybe even a twin with the Big Spruce colt sold at aution, and Whitney made a figurative killing, if not a literal one. Phelps told Monk that the whole story would be the subject of Sunday's Louisville Courier Journal. Even if he got some slick lawyer to keep him out of jail, Landis would suffer great punishment. All that was important to entitled assholes like him was related to his status in social circles.

In the state of Kentucky, in the rarified social air of horse breeding aristocracy like the DuPonts, the Seagram family heirs, Nelson Bunker Hunt, the Hancocks of Claiborne Farm, and the Wrights of Calumet Farm all of whose money and influence Whitney Landis needed to be governor, or county dog catcher for that matter, the breeding and betting scandal soon attached to the Landis name would render him a leper in those social circles, and all the power and money needed for his political career would vanish. Whitney was toast.

So, Monk thought, like most events in the lives of both good and bad people, this saga would end, not with T.S. Eliot's satisfactory bang, but maybe with something slightly louder than a whimper.

www.ingramcontent.com/pod-product-compliance
Lightning Source LLC
Chambersburg PA
CBHW022157160726
48282CB00024B/233

* 9 7 8 9 3 9 5 1 3 1 0 4 9 *